Joanne Banyer

AWAKENING III

Eternal Love

Joanne ✻ Banyer
Awakening for Humanity

AWAKENING III - Eternal Love
First published by AWAKENING FOR HUMANITY 2025
ABN 82415992557
Website: https://www.awakeningforhumanity.com

YouTube: https://www.youtube.com/@awakeningforhumanity
Facebook: https://www.facebook.com/joanne.banyer.2025/
Instagram: https://www.instagram.com/awakeningforhumanity/

Copyright © Joanne Banyer 2025

A pre-publication data record for this title is available
from The National Library of Australia.

ISBN: 978-1-7635979-8-3 (Paperback)
ISBN: 978-1-7635979-9-0 (Hardback)
ISBN: 978-1-7643430-0-8 (ePub e-book)
ISBN: 978-1-7643430-1-5 (Audiobook)

The right of Joanne Banyer to be identified as author of this work
has been asserted by the author in accordance with sections 77
and 78 of the Copyright, Designs and Patents Act 1988.

All rights reserved. No part of this publication may be reproduced, stored in a
retrieval system, or transmitted in any form or by any means, electronic, mechanical,
photocopying, recording, or otherwise, without the prior permission of the author.

Any person who commits any unauthorised act in relation to this publication
may be liable to criminal prosecution and civil claims for damages.

All of the events in this memoir are true to the best of the author's memory. The views
expressed in this memoir are solely those of the author unless otherwise noted.

For my mother, Gwendoline Barbara Banyer.
My role model, my mentor, my protector in physical life.

I have never met someone who so fiercely protects her children from everyone and everything—even at the age of 87. I often joke with Mum that she is just like Ma Kettle out of the 1940s and 50s film, and later comic film series, *Ma and Pa Kettle*. It was about a pair of hillbillies who had their hands full with a ramshackle farm and brood of rambunctious children. Ma Kettle was often depicted in a rocking chair with a shot gun, willing to blow away anything that got her goat. My mum is incredibly defensive of *her* children. They can do no wrong even when they do. I love you, Mum. You are precious.

She is part of the team now—working alongside me, editing each book, and wanting to be a part of bringing this series to the world. Mum is often full of questions and curiosity about my antics with Spirit and where things are up to. Her reaction when I showed her a paperback version of the first book, was tangible. I nearly had to catch her as she stumbled. She was full of emotion. She knew how long it had taken me to get to that moment—my unwavering determination to do justice by all that I experience, and why.

This one's for you.

Your loving daughter
Joanne
xox

Joanne is an ordinary person, having an extraordinary experience. She first encountered Spirit at the age of six. Later, Spirit wanted Joanne to know it exists beyond doubt when her father unexpectedly died in January 2014. Four years later, out of the blue, Spirit made its presence known in a profound way that changed Joanne's life forever. Since then, Spirit has become a part of her everyday life, where she balances family and work in areas of Australia's national security, with an ever-evolving journey of spiritual awakening.

This true story is based on Joanne's personal encounters with Spirit, the recordings of which started in a journal gifted from her son at Christmas in 2016. There are eleven books in the *AWAKENING* series, which are all based on Joanne's personal journals. The books are called:

- *I - The Beginning*
- *II - 1NF1N1T1*
- *III - Eternal Love*
- *IV - This I Know, This Time Around*
- *V - Esoteric Lifetime*
- *VI - Ascension*
- *VII - Kundalini*
- *VIII - Becoming*
- *IX - Ascension Access*
- *X - Luminescent Transcendence*
- *XI - Revenant Indemnification*

How these names came about is unique, each appearing before, then becoming a theme in the journal. Certainly, spiritually influenced!

In 2024, Joanne launched the *awakeningforhumanity.com* website and an online *AWAKENING* Research Community space, which includes an information hub and collaboration space for those experiencing awakening, researching this phenomenon or who are fascinated in the subject. Joanne's longer-term goal is to build a global following in her story of awakening and attract donations to fund the associated research. Joanne is interested to hear from scientists and bright sparks, who research the existence of Spirit energy, and those with knowledge in areas of science who study the detection and characterisation of unknown sources of energy—space-time and wormholes, including quantum physics and sacred geometry and cymatics. Joanne can be contacted by email on joanne@awakeningforhumanity.com. She is not looking to scientists to believe in spirit energy; she is looking to them to prove its existence beyond doubt for the sake of humanity.

AWAKENING Research Community Space now available at awakeningforhumanity.com

Over the past six years I've come to realise that millions of people around the world are, or have, experienced spiritual awakening, and there is a growing number of scientists, researchers and bright sparks trying to understand and prove it. Essentially, research that is essential to understanding the other half of ourselves. The non-physical part, which plays just as critical a role in our existence and purpose of being, as the physical part. Without this knowledge, this proof, humanity will continue to blindly evolve, not understanding fully what we are and why we are here, not keeping up with the potential that our intelligence, our evolution of consciousness, now affords us.

The online AWAKENING Research Community Space is a way to bring people together who experience and research the awakening phenomena.

It provides a free, safe, and supportive place to share information and collaborate to build our knowledge about awakening. By joining the community, you'll not only contribute to a deeper understanding of awakening, but also find others walking a similar path.

Together, we can learn, grow, and inspire one another on this journey.

I'd love for you to be part of it.

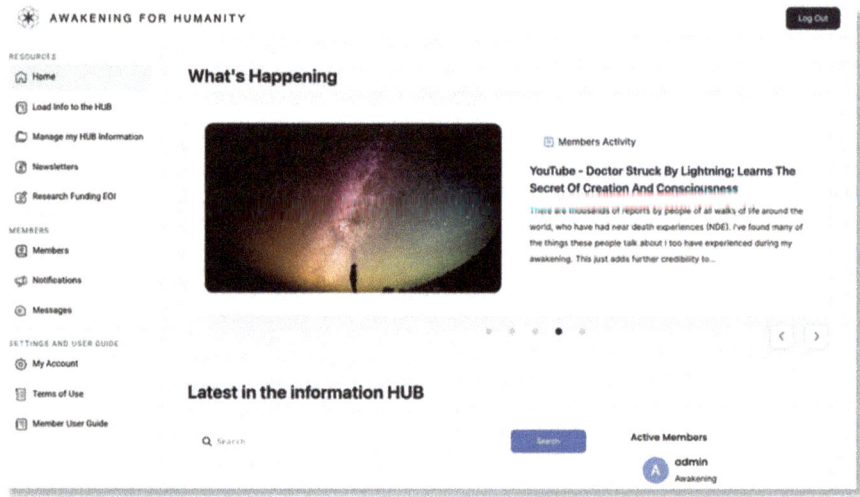

Acknowledgments

Thank you, Jamie, for giving me the first journal. And John, for the encouragement to write the journals up as a book series. Without you, this true personal account would never have been shared. Thank you, Warick, for your love, protection and perseverance with me. This is our journey, the most challenging of which lies ahead of us. Thank you, Elder and Jules, for being wise and saying the right things at the right time.

Thank you to all online sources, particularly those who post *YouTube* videos, where there is a large community of people wanting to share their personal experiences with Spirit in the hope of helping others to understand what it is they experience. Spiritual awakening can be a lonely journey, where mainstream sources of information are inadequate. Although much online content is not peer reviewed, as the journals will show, collectively it has served as a dictionary from which Spirit draws my attention to information. Usually, it is only snippets of information at a time from a handful of sources, which collectively builds a picture to help me understand, or reinforce something they want me to know. Awakening is a learning and development process.

Special thanks go to the following published sources who have generously provided permission for me to refer to, and quote, their authors' work:

- Llewellyn Publications Woodbury, Minnesota – permission to use material from 'DESTINY OF SOULS: New Case Studies of Life Between Lives' authored by Michael Newton, PhD.
- Seth Center, New Awareness Network Inc. Manhasset, New York – permission to use material from 'A SETH BOOK, THE EARLY SESSIONS, Book 6 of The Seth Material'.

This book is unique in every way.

What started as desire for my awakening journey to be communicated in a variety of ways to resonate with as many people as possible, soon transitioned to wanting the following artists to share their own personal reaction to the story through the art they create for each book in the series. A glimpse into their own life's journey and how mine affected theirs when painting the cover for a book, composing a theme song and meditation track for the audio versions, drawing a portrait of a key Spirit character, composing a poem, and developing a 3D animated mini-movie. Thank you for being willing to walk this journey with me, offering your creations to what will be a series of *AWAKENING* books.

John Mallory – Paranormal Investigator

John is a paranormal investigator, who lives in Vancouver, British Columbia, Canada. He is the founder of White Light Paranormal www.whitelightparanormal.com and the inventor of the Panabox spirit radio. He manages *The Panabox & Panasonic DR60 Users Forum* Facebook group and travels the world in search of paranormal phenomena.

John was first contacted by Joanne when she learned of his Panabox through a *YouTube* video created by Life After Death/ITC Innovator, Steve Huff. During their initial conversation, John learned of Joanne's unique and profound spiritual experiences and felt an inner need to gift her several paranormal detection devices, including a Panabox. He then suggested she contact spiritual medium, Jules Stirling, for spiritual guidance.

Over the next few months, Joanne shared with John her ongoing experiences with Spirit, which she diligently records in journals. He was so fascinated with what she had written that he suggested she consider publishing her work. In subsequent months, titles for each journal 'magically' popped up in John's head and were offered to Joanne. Through the course of writing in a journal, she found these titles to become highly significant to the experiences she was having. The two have continued this pattern of communication to this day where Joanne is continuing her journey with Spirit in a next series called ACCESS.

Fiber – Online Marketing
A Canberra based, odd ball group of online marketers, designers and developers who are impetuously impassioned about finding your digital personality.

www.fiber.com.au

In December 2023, Joanne found a team willing to work with her in marketing and promoting the series. She was in it for the long haul and wanted to give the series the very best opportunity for success. Joanne's goal was to build a global following of the story. Lucky for her, Fiber was prepared to join her on this journey. The selling point for Joanne was their dog, Cookie, who appears on their website as the last member of their team. Cookie knew Joanne when they first met. Meant to be, she thinks. Cookie honours Joanne by his photo being the first piece of data in the online *AWAKENING* Research Community 'Information Hub' at awakeningforhumanity.com, where people can become a member and use the 'Information Hub' and collaboration features for free. She couldn't let the Fiber team remove it when it was used as a piece of dummy data when the site was in development. Cookie is Information Hub's very own mascot.

Catherine Hiller – Abstract Expressionist Artist

Catherine is an abstract expressionist artist whose work concentrates on powerful, emotional moments in time. Through very energetic and sensual strokes, she expresses her love of paint and colour.

Her works are raw and visceral, the product of instinct rather than intellect. Being very sensitive to her surroundings, every cue, whether visual, aural or emotional, has a colour, which Catherine translates onto canvas without the distraction of a thought process.

French born, Catherine studied art in Paris before embarking on a successful career in advertising in the UK. After eleven years in the UK, she moved to Australia in 2004 and has been living in Melbourne since. Catherine has had solo and group shows in France, England and Australia, and her work is represented in private collections around the world.

For more information about Catherine Hiller, visit her website –

www.catherinehiller.com or email *info@catherinehiller.com*

Cedric Vermue—Composer and Pianist

Cedric is a composer and pianist. Music is an intuitive tool. It expresses what is close to his heart.

Based in the countryside next to Amsterdam, Cedric lives a quiet life with apple trees in his garden, and the barn transformed into a music recording studio.

He never promoted himself as a healing musician, but he is very conscious and grateful for the healing and connecting abilities that music offers us, and its meditative and therapeutic quality. Cedric made it his life mission to create and offer this musical expression to the world.

His music can be found online on Spotify, *YouTube* and other platforms. The music he composes for the *AWAKENING* series can be purchased from https://cedricvermue.bandcamp.com

You can get in touch through his Instagram *@cedricvermue*.

Marie Klement—Spirit Artist

Marie is a Spirit artist, who sketched Wolf, who is featured in this book.

Based in South Australia, Marie has a special ability to take communications a step further by linking with Spirit and transmitting onto paper an image of a person's Spirit guide, angel, divinity, or passed away loved one that she is psychically in touch with. Spirit artists are mediums, who are influenced to draw or paint art by the spirit world.

Marie is mainly self-taught and works full time as a spirit artist, medium and numerologist.

Marie has demonstrated her extraordinary talents with TV's, *Sensing Murder* psychic, Scott Russell Hill, as well as UK mediums, Lisa Williams and Tony Stockwell.

For more information about Marie Klement, visit her website – *www.marieklement.com.au* or Facebook site – *Marie Klement and Marie Klement Spirit Art*. Marie can be contacted by email on *mkvisionart@gmail.com*.

Marlene Seven Bremner—Esoteric themed poet, painter and author
Seven was born in Frankfurt, Germany in 1983 and moved to the US at the age of four. She is a self-taught oil painter, author and poet, exploring esoteric themes arising from her study and practice of hermeticism, alchemy, tarot, psychology, magic, astrology, shamanism, and mythology.

Seven developed her career in the Pacific Northwest of the US, showing her artwork in both group and solo exhibitions along the West Coast and writing on-the-spot poetry at local markets as part of a Poem Store. She relocated to New Mexico in 2019, where she lives a hermetic lifestyle and continues to paint and write.

Seven's subject matter has been greatly influenced by Jungian psychology and alchemical philosophy, both of which have provided her with a symbolic language to interpret otherwise ineffable sensations and impressions. Alchemy is the understanding of how consciousness relates to matter, which Seven has explored in-depth through the creative process. As physical, mental and emotional transmutation takes place within, it is projected externally onto the canvas or into a poem, distilling a psycho-spiritual process into its creative quintessence. The aim of the alchemical work, called the *Magnum Opus*, is to free the authentic self to be in alignment with its perfect, divine, unified nature, and to awaken the creative potential and power of the human imagination.

More information about Marlene Seven Bremner's art and writing can be found on her website at *marlenesevenbremner.com*. She has a Facebook page at *Marlene Seven Bremner – Art* and Instagram page @ *m7artist*. Seven can also be reached by email at *sevenbremner@gmail.com*. Her books are available from Inner Traditions.

Larimar Sound Alchemy—Meditation Sound Therapist

Larimar is a sound therapist based in London, who creates sound alchemy for relaxation, healing, shamanic journeying, inspiration of inner vision, and empowerment. Most of Larimar's music is live recorded sound meditations composed of vocal harmonics and healing instruments, such as the gong, Tibetan and crystal singing bowls, didgeridoo, berimbau, chakapa, drums, and flute. Larimar's fascination with music and sound begun in his early childhood, where hearing his own voice played back to him from a cassette recorder absolutely blew his mind. This led to recording stories as they played out in his mind as a little kid, on a tape recorder gifted from his grandmother, playing around on his mother's guitar, jamming with friends in a local park, and these days writing and recording music in his home studio. Introduction to the plant medicine called Ayahuasca in 2010, was a key moment in his life that inspired him to study shamanism, systematic kinesiology, neurokinetic therapy, and Reiki. Spending many years working with plant medicines, Larimar has observed and studied the healing abilities of music and song. In parallel, during his practice of Capoeira (an Afro-Brazilian art form combining martial arts, music and philosophy), Larimar noticed similarities with the ritualistic use of rhythm and singing, and the effects it had on his well-being. Larimar considers sound healing to be an easily accessible and very effective form of complementary therapy that yields profound results in helping people restore well-being. Through therapeutic application of vocals and instruments, a state of deep relaxation can be achieved. In this state of meditative awareness, not only are stress and stored emotions released, but also harmony and clarity are restored. You can find out more about Larimar by visiting *https://larimarsound.com/*.

Alexandre Roesner Lino—3D Animation Film Producer

Alexandre is passionate about science, art, and nature, which inspire much of his work. Born on an island in southern Brazil, surrounded by beaches and lush forests, Alexandre has always been deeply connected to nature. The waves and surfing have been a lifelong passion, providing moments of calm and inspiration for his creative endeavours. In contrast to his love for nature, technology has also been a significant part of his life, and from an early age, he knew it was his professional calling. Despite studying Electrical Engineering, art led him down an irreversible path. In 2002, he founded his solo enterprise, Terramidia (with 'Terra' meaning 'Earth' in Portuguese). Combining his love for art and technology, he dedicated many years to studying 3D animation, producing numerous films and commercials for individuals and companies worldwide, a pursuit he continues to this day with great enthusiasm. The world of 3D animation is vast and ever evolving, with endless opportunities for learning and growth. Perfection seems an elusive goal. Following the success of some of his digital characters, he has become known as 'The Alien Guy'. You can view his work on his website, *YouTube* and social media platforms.

YouTube: https://www.youtube.com/@terramidia3d
Website: https://www.terramidia3d.com/
Instagram: https://www.instagram.com/terramidia3d

Alex and Joanne collaborate in the production of mini movies for each *AWAKENING* series book for only 3D animation can show the richness of the astounding things that Joanne experiences in non-physical realms. Joanne hopes one day a mainstream movie producer will want to base a movie series on the *AWAKENING* series, thereby reaching more people around the world with this incredible true story. *AWAKENING* series mini movies can be viewed at https://www.youtube.com/@awakeningforhumanity

Table of Contents

Preface i

6 January 2021 1

7 January 2021 3

8 January 2021 5

9 January 2021 9

10 January 2021 10

12 January 2021 12

14 January 2021 14

17 January 2021 16

20 January 2021 17

22 January 2021 20

26 January 2021 22

28 January 2021 25

31 January 2021 26

1 February 2021 27

3 February 2021 28

13 February 2021 29

14 February 2021 31

18 February 2021 33

28 February 2021 34

3 March 2021 38

4 March 2021 40

5 March 2021 42

8 March 2021 44

17 March 2021 46

18 March 2021	47
22 March 2021	49
24 March 2021	51
26 March 2021	53
30 March 2021	55
31 March 2021	56
4 April 2021	57
6 April 2021	59
10 April 2021	61
11 April 2021	62
13 April 2021	63
14 April 2021	64
17 April 2021	65
18 April 2021	67
29 April 2021	69
3 May 2021	71
4 May 2021	74
5 May 2021	76
7 May 2021	77
15 May 2021	79
17 May 2021	80
20 May 2021	81
21 May 2021	82
22 May 2021	83
25 May 2021	84
4 June 2021	85
5 June 2021	88
9 June 2021	90
10 June 2021	91

14 June 2021 ... 93
15 June 2021 ... 97
17 June 2021 ... 98
22 June 2021 ... 100
23 June 2021 ... 102
29 June 2021 ... 103
7 July 2021 ... 104
8 July 2021 ... 109
9 July 2021 ... 110
11 July 2021 ... 112
13 July 2021 ... 114
14 July 2021 ... 117
15 July 2021 ... 121
17 July 2021 ... 123
18 July 2022 ... 124
20 July 2021 ... 127
21 July 2021 ... 128
22 July 2021 ... 129
23 July 2021 ... 131
24 July 2021 ... 132
25 July 2021 ... 134
29 July 2021 ... 135
5 August 2021 ... 137
8 August 2021 ... 138
9 August 2021 ... 141
10 August 2021 ... 146
11 August 2021 ... 147

Preface

Well, Jamie, by now if you have read these journals, you may think your mother has an amazing imagination, is completely looney, is having a mid-life crisis, is suffering from symptoms of perimenopause, or is having an incredible experience with the spirit world that probably few have recorded as I have.

I hope I haven't lost you in this yet. It will be interesting to see what John proposes for the title of this book. I hope he does. I like his contribution in this way. He is a part of the journey now and at this stage he is the only human who knows it all. I haven't lost him yet, so there is still hope for Warick and my quest—to communicate to the masses that intelligent energy beyond what we know exists, and with the help of the scientific community, maybe one day, also prove it beyond any possible doubt. Then there is hope for all.

As always, I love you with all my heart.

Mum xox

A Body of Eternal Love
By Marlene Seven Bremner

*Waves of longing
break upon the endless shore,
as Aurora gleams hopeful
through morning dew
and everywhere, evermore,
the shadow shapes
of you,
abiding love beyond
the bounds of sight—*

*You, who come
so sweetly in the night,
this undulating sea
rising and falling
by your gentle wind,
a tickle in the throat
awakens the sapphire
flower of your voice
finding its power
to speak,
and my heart,
a flaming poppy
unfurling at dawn,
deep rooted burning
to be One—*

*To share this vessel
in service to Spirit,
a Body of Eternal Love
for you to inhabit,
Soul seeing by the Falcon's eye
piercing Saturn's rings
of time,
enveloped in sublime
cerulean light
Body, Soul, and Mind
aligned with the infinite.*

6 January 2021

In the United Kingdom, one in fifty people have COVID-19. Yesterday, they had sixty thousand new cases in one day, outstripping their fifty thousand new cases in one day about a week ago.

Lately, I've had a couple of interesting experiences during meditation, which I think I should record but I don't know if they are true. I certainly have never pre-thought what may occur during meditation, except on one occasion when wanting to see either Warick or Elder, or both. I've never thought about what the encounters may entail, except for a possible question or two that I'd like to ask if the opportunity came up. What occurs during meditation literally unfolds in the moment. I let the thoughts run through my mind. If what I experience is true, or partly true, then the events of late are significant. I'm starting to wonder if Warick is using these times as an opportunity to regress me to the life I lived when I was with him in a physical life—where our bond formed, and where Elder became a significant guide for us in our physical lives. Yesterday, I just wanted to see Elder. It started by my seeing a sketch of an elderly native American Indian male on *YouTube*. The *YouTube* video is called 'Native American Sleep Music: canyon flute and nocturnal canyon sounds' by Nu Meditation Music. This sketch immediately made me think of Elder. I wanted to visit him. When I went to bed, I listened to the Tibetan Bells Healing Sounds meditation track by Meditation and Relaxation, where I've met up with Warick and Elder previously. During the meditation, I leaned over Elder's body, who was laid out on a raised platform in a cave. He was dying. I was talking to him. Warick was standing away and behind me. No one else was there. Elder looked at me and said, 'Eternal'. I knew he was about to pass. In desperation I said, 'You leave me here, you come to me there' (meaning my current physical life). I didn't want to lose him. I love him very much and value everything he has been teaching me. He looked at me and said with his mind, 'I will never leave you, Joanne'. I was surprised that he used my current physical life's name. I was annoyed that Warick wasn't closer and trying to do something. I felt despair and heartache. We burned Elder's body that night. The next day, while sitting in front of Warick on his horse, he walked the horse very slowly around the edge of the canyon's cliff. I felt completely lost, empty and sad. Interestingly, about a week ago, during meditation, I saw my own death when I was a native American Indian woman. I don't know the significance of being shown Elder's and my death in close succession. I died of old age. I remember holding a blanket around me, wandering out into the wilderness, then crouching against some large rocks. By morning I had died, alone. Warick, who had already passed away, came to meet me in spirit form. He looked young, handsome and peaceful. My son at the time, who I think is Jamie (my son in this lifetime), came looking for me on his horse and retrieved my body. That's all I remember.

I've been missing Warick lately. He seems to be focusing on merging with me in different ways. I'm wondering if this takes quite a lot of his energy. More than what he uses to stimulate my senses with vibrations. I'll have to ask Jane Hall, a medium I've visited a few times in Canberra. I think Warick knows I've been missing him because this morning I woke to pulse sounds to greet me, and some vibrations, although scaled down significantly compared with the usual energy sensations I experience in different parts of my body.

7 January 2021

A personal moment. It's hard to know whether to put this in the journal or not. Warick is with me now. He touched the right side of my cheek when I asked, 'Should I write about this?' It was not a convincing response. Then again, he has just come through with a lot stronger touch on the right cheek, and again now, so I suppose he agrees that yes, I should write about this. Today I saw Jane again. The picture is building. Consciously, Jane has very much accepted what she has experienced lifetime after lifetime. Persecution of the worst kind. In this life, Jane is highly connected to the spirit world and has experienced persecution for having spiritual abilities in many other lifetimes. In this lifetime, I sense she feels uncomfortable and is avoiding taking on a mentoring and teaching role to help me connect with Spirit in trance mediumship. Instead, she focuses her services on helping people to transform their lives. She said she doesn't want to specialise in trance mediumship and is pulling away from the spiritual work. She wants to help people heal from grief. It's strange, but the first few times I met with Jane it's almost like she was frightened of a path to teach me. She seemed very mixed about helping me. It's almost like she is still feeling crucified and is still running. Still hiding what she is. I will stay connected to Jane, and like John, I hope over time the relationship, or my contribution to it in some small way, will help her. I sense there is a lot going on in her mind when it comes to us. It's okay, and I want her to feel safe with me. I want this more than anything. For several months now I've also wanted John to feel safe with me. Recently, John said he can accept that he and I are meant to help each other. The signs and ways our guides are using us to help each other has been so obvious. Warick just touched my left cheek meaning he disagrees, but I'm not sure why.

I'm wondering if Jules is Elder reincarnated. I suspected months ago that she is a wise one who says what needs to be said at the right time. I also have in my mind what Elder said just before he died—'I will never leave you, Joanne'. I've had a strong feeling that he would show up in my current physical life. We shall see. Warick is touching my left cheek now, so I suspect I have this wrong. And he just touched my left cheek again, and now my right cheek, so I suspect my thoughts here are wrong and he is agreeing with me understanding him. That's okay. Hopefully Elder will show up again in meditation or life. That's fine. I love him and miss him. Life is complex. Just when I think I have worked something out, I get the lovely touch on the cheek to say, 'Actually, no, you are wrong.' I love it! It makes me smile. My life is so much more interesting with you in it, Warick, which I'm sure you know.

Checking notes that I made during a meeting with Jane, she said a couple of other interesting things worth including here. She said most trance mediums have a child that comes through. I find this interesting because possibly this is the spirit child Phil senses around me. I asked her about a comment she made about Warick being an enlightened spirit. She said it is a knowing that she had at the time. She also said what I am experiencing is light trance, where I'm conscious that Spirit is there, but they are aside. Trance is a half-conscious state.

8 January 2021

I had a terrific session with Jules today. I discovered that she practices trance meditation every week. I think she will be an excellent sounding board to talk to about what I'm experiencing, to help me navigate where Warick may be guiding me to. There were plenty of interesting things we discussed today. She thinks I may be trance writing when I'm writing in my journal. I think that might be right much of the time. Warick is usually with me as I write, including now. I can feel him in my right cheek, but he is trying not to be too obvious about it today. Trance writing would explain why I write very fluently. The words just come, and I write them down. I rarely spend any time thinking about it. Sometimes, when I go to make a note about something I want to write in the journal later, I just keep writing. Also, when I typed up the first journal recently, I found I barely needed to make any changes, except minor editing and sentence construction. Essentially, what I wrote in the journal remained largely untouched. It makes sense that I could be trance writing. It's a joint effort with Spirit. I know that.

Warick is with me a lot of the time day and night, which I love and am very comfortable with. I miss him when he's not here. That said, I'm also happy to go about my physical life each day, but I'm even happier when Warick pops in and makes himself known to me. I just say hi, tell him how much I appreciate and love him being there, and then get on with whatever I'm doing. Feeling Warick within me is normal now, as well as often catching a glimpse of him as a shadow shape moving around me.

In this entry, I also want to describe what just happened when I tried trance during meditation with no music or guidance. I just had my earplugs in to block out distracting noises. Warick was there immediately, as he usually is when I start to meditate. I first felt him on my right cheek, and then he very gently touched my mouth. It was very subtle. Very quickly he showed me men walking up a hill in single file. All had backpacks on, and all were dressed as native American Indians. It was a still image initially. I thought I was walking behind someone and then thought maybe I'm Warick walking behind another man. I thought maybe Warick wants me to describe what I'm seeing, to get things going by way of his possibly speaking through me. Jules said today that she finds she has to say a few words to get things going, and then the words come from Spirit. I started to do this, just focusing on describing what I could see. And then, just like during meditation when I'm with Warick and Elder, other things started to happen. Falcon came into view. He was flying overhead. I also saw Wolf and I said, 'Wolf is following to keep an eye on me (my spirit within Warick) because you (Warick) are not here'. It was only men, and they were on a deer hunting trip to get food. The weather was bad. It was snowing. The scene then moved to nighttime where the men were around a campfire, happy and playing a flute, with Wolf in the background keeping an eye on things.

The scene then moved to the next day, walking down the hill in better weather with deer in hand, and children running out from the village to greet us. Warick wanted to bathe so he went to the river where I (my native American Indian woman self) joined him. Warick's thoughts were what I (myself in this life) spoke during the mediation. About how he thinks I'm beautiful, cheeky, and how strong we are together. The scene then moved to nighttime where the village people were celebrating around a fire while eating barbequed deer, and the men were smoking pipes. The scene ended with Warick and I naked, lying together in furs in a tent and Warick thinking how smooth my skin was. Through this entire experience, I thought what Warick thought and spoke it as a whisper. I experienced the scene through Warick's eyes. I could feel Warick across my face the entire time. I didn't experience the state of being completely merged with him. I do question whether this was all my imagination, but just like the meditation sessions, it seemed very fluid. A few times I think my own thoughts started to interrupt a bit, but I tried to back out as this happened, which seemed to work. I certainly did not pre-think the scenes that occurred, nor my experience of seeing them through Warick's eyes and knowing his thoughts. It's the first time this has happened. Something I didn't even know was possible. What confirmed it for me was when I was him looking at me in the water when he bathed. A touch on the right cheek now from Warick confirms this perspective. He is so clever in his thinking of how to take someone like me, with my fear (only slight) of him talking through me and turn it into comfort. Instead of his spirit talking through me, he got my spirit to see through his eyes, know his thoughts, and speak to them as they came to mind. Essentially, he reversed what I've been frightened of, to give me some sense of what it's like with my spirit speaking through him.

Something else I want to make a note of today, is my fear of the connection I have with John. Warick is lightly touching my right cheek now in agreement. I sensed that John was not comfortable when initially, I was very open and shared things with both Jules and him. He never responded his thoughts to both of us, only in correspondence with just me. He seemed more comfortable with my complete openness and sharing with him only. I learned this early on, and for months now I've continued this approach, which I love and wouldn't change for anything. We are growing together. Not together as such, but rather walking our own paths, side by side, sharing our experiences, in our own ways, and our guides are definitely leveraging this for each of our own benefits. We now see and accept that we are helping each other. I don't want this to change, and Warick has lightly touched my right cheek now to confirm this. I'm concerned about how John will go when for the first time we live stream online with Jules and Jane. His conscious mind is so wary of me. I know this and try to be very careful with how I engage him so as not to spook him, so to speak. I feel lately there is a growing trust between us where he says he believes what I write. Maybe he is just being supportive, but I don't think so. I believe him. I think the answer is that I will just be upfront and honest about what I'm concerned about. Warick is trying very hard not to touch my right cheek now to agree with me and is settling for some presence around the top of my nose. I know he agrees with me. I need to be careful and not get too cocky or confident as I suspect it will bite me on the bum. This all matters very much. No matter what, John will remain my confidant as long as he is comfortable and wants to do this. Warick touched my right cheek again now, agreeing with this. Our paths are intertwined.

9 January 2021

Record of experience while doing a 'Sitting in the Power' meditation session

One hour. No music. Ear plugs. Sitting up on bed. Felt myself nodding off numerous times. I experienced what felt like a very distinct cobweb come over the back right of my head and stay there for a bit. This took me by surprise, so I probably jolted a bit. I heard a single tone and pressure in my left ear a couple of times, which occurred pretty close together and not too loud. I felt tingling in the usual places most of the time, and outside my root chakra several times. I saw no scenes through Warick's eyes like I did yesterday. There was no attempt to speak through me. Pretty boring really.

10 January 2021

Record of experience while doing a 'Sitting in the Power' meditation session

Same setting and conditions as on 9 January 2021.

I nodded off a few times. I focused on feeling the tingling at my feet, root chakra and head throughout most of the session. I brought my mind back to this when it wandered off. Just before the end of the session I felt something touching the right outer edge of my breast and arm. It tickled, which made me open my eyes eventually to see what it was in case it was a spider sitting on me. I'm not fond of spiders. I felt very warm at one stage, and it felt like Warick was merged with me at the time, but he wasn't interested in talking. I heard a long tone in my right ear at one point.

Resumed journal entries.

It's like I have this insatiable appetite for Spirit encounters. Warick is touching my right cheek now in agreement. I do feel sorry for Warick, Elder and any other guides I may have. I must be a handful. And another touch on my right cheek from Warick. I feel sad or a bit down when I don't have special moments and experiences with Warick. And another touch on my right cheek from Warick. It's the emotion I feel for him. I can't help it. And another touch on the right cheek. I also once again don't feel like I'm progressing by way of development of psychic and medium abilities. I feel like I'm opening myself up to it, making myself available and doing all I can, but nothing. Tonight, while having fish and chips with Ray's friends at Lake Burley Griffin in Canberra, I thought to myself that 'Sitting in the Power' meditation, unguided and with no music, is just like fishing. You sit, and you wait. And you sit, and you wait. And you sit, and you wait. Very still, very quiet, and nothing, and nothing, and nothing. I had so much more going on by way of experiences doing the meditation tracks I found myself, or that Warick guided me to. What others say about doing 'Sitting in the Power' regularly so Spirit can learn how to match your vibration to enable engagement with you, I'm not sure will help me. Up until now, there's plenty to suggest that I'm plugged into the spirit dimension most of the time, such as tingling sensations when I'm sitting and walking around. Spirit also tends to pop in and out of my body at will. The 'what more' that I want and have been hoping for all along, is to see and communicate with Spirit and now also to be able to channel Warick. I'm keeping a record of what I experience during 'Sitting in the Power' sessions in a separate book, which I'll include when I type up the journal. I don't think I've provided a summary of my sessions with Jane and Jules this past week, which I'll include in the next entry. A touch on the right cheek from Warick suggests that I haven't.

The world continues to be crazy. Trump supporters stormed the National Capital Building in Washington, D.C. Four people died, and over fifty people were arrested. Although he has less than two weeks to go in office, he is likely to face impeachment.

12 January 2021

Poor Warick. I feel so sorry for him—kind of. I just spent the first fifteen minutes of a no music, no guidance 'Sitting in the Power' session having a really good talk to him. I'm sure if there is a God, Warick is now issuing a complaint that this is enough, and he wants out! No further contact with me. I felt a very slight touch on the right cheek just now, and again now, indicating some level of agreement with me. I suppose I carried on to Warick about this whole sitting in a circle thing in one month's time, and there being no indication so far that we are in any way ready for it. That is, if he wants to talk through me, which he confirmed with touches on the right cheek. 'Sitting in the Power' at the moment is 'Fing' boring. As I said to John in an email today, I feel like I'm fishing—literally. Waiting, waiting, waiting, with not much happening. Especially compared with all the other exciting things that have happened. I know Warick has needed to work on me physically, mentally and emotionally to get me to a point where he can talk through me or facilitate Elder coming through. But for people like Jules and Jane, I wonder have they gone through this type of preparation? I honestly don't know. Jane said for her it is like riding a bike. I do get that. For Jules, I haven't asked. Right now, I honestly don't think I care. I've opened myself up to it. I've been a stuffed dummy sitting there, waiting to be occupied. And so far, it's been pretty uneventful.

Okay, now that I've blown off some steam and given up after fifteen minutes of 'Sitting in the Power', I'll record a few other things I do think are worth noting. The other night I just wanted comfort, so I listened to a howling winds storm meditation track. I met up with Elder again, which was just wonderful. It said to me that even though I witnessed his death, I can still engage with him in the native American Indian form. It suggests that I'm either living that existence in that dimension at the same time as this existence, which Jules suggested and is possibly right, or time doesn't matter, and I can be taken to different moments in a lifetime before and after witnessing death of individuals. At the moment, I'm leaning towards Jules's thoughts. Anyway, during the howling wind meditation, Elder and I were standing side by side, looking out across the canyon at the storm and lightening. He said to me, 'You know it's not just the chemicals in the rain that make the plants grow so well. It's also the raindrops being electrically charged with energy.' I've never heard this before. It's a wonderful concept. I've always taken notice of just how well plants stand up and respond to rainwater compared with water which is chemically treated by humans. They really do look like they are more alive and have more energy so to speak.

The other day I was trying to explain to Mum, while drawing on my memory of what I'd read quite some time ago in the Seth series, how you are made up of different conscious states that deal with the physical world, dream states and deeper levels of consciousness. I must have stuffed it up because that night, when I couldn't sleep at one o'clock in the morning, I opened my kindle to continue reading the Seth series, and hey presto, Warick had led me to a section where, for some reason, Seth revisited this subject providing a really good description of it. He said it depends where your focus is. That is the dimension you're interacting with, whether that be something in the physical world, a dream or the spiritual dimension. Anyway, it was terrific, and of course I had to read it to Mum, while also explaining that Warick had brought this to my attention, obviously not happy with the explanation I provided to her the day before.

I have other things to write about by way of my session with Jules the other day, but I'm tired so want to stop. But before I do, I will mention my highlight of the day. John sent me a message to say he has started seeing shadow shapes in his peripheral vision. I'm so excited! I can't help my enthusiasm. I'm so happy for him. As I said to him, I suspect they are your guides. After all the years John has focused on the spirit world, I'm just so happy that his connection with Spirit is starting to happen in a way that his conscious mind is aware and accepting of. Super exciting! If nothing further happens on my path, and in some small way I helped this connection for John, then my job is done. And I couldn't be happier. Tonight, I'm over the moon!!!

14 January 2021

Question and Answer session with Warick, with cheek responses

Note - I tried using the pendulum; however, Warick went straight to using touches on my cheeks to provide the answers. Right cheek means yes and left cheek no. I didn't continue with the pendulum.

- Is my relationship with Jane to continue for mutual benefit? Yes
- Is my relationship with Jules to continue for mutual benefit? No response
- Is my relationship with John to continue for mutual benefit? Yes
- Do you want to use me for trance mediumship? Yes
- Do you want to use me for trance writing ability? No (answer slow, not clear)
- Do you love me? Yes
- Will you continue to walk this path with me no matter what? Yes
- Do you want me to write what you say through trance mediumship? Yes
- Will you talk through me? Yes and No
- Will you talk through members of the circle and not just me? No
- Will you only talk through me? Not clear
- Will you also talk through Jane? Yes
- Will you talk through Jules? Yes
- Will you talk through John? No
- Will you talk through me? Yes
- Will you talk through me when we first sit in the circle with John, Jules, and Jane? No
- If we sit in a circle again together, will you talk through me? Yes
- Will Ray stick with me through this no matter what? Yes
- Will I be able to do something to prove this to him eventually? No response

- Is my purpose to write what you say? Yes
- Am I just a vehicle to speak through, record what you say and publish it? Yes
- Were we a couple in the past? Yes
- Is that why we have a strong and trusted bond? Yes
- Is Jules a part of my future path? Yes
- Is Elder one of Jules's guides? Yes and No
- Is Jules soul Elder? Yes and No
- Is Jules one part of Elder? Yes
- Is Elder reincarnated through Jules now? Yes and No
- Is Elder a guide of Jules? Yes
- Is Elder Jules's higher self? Yes and No
- Is Elder a guide of Jules? Not clear
- Warick, do you love me? Yes
- Do you love me as we were when native American Indians? Yes and No
- Do you also love me for who I am now? Yes and No
- When I meditate do you take me back to a previous incarnation? No
- When I meditate, do you take me to another dimension of my spirit's existence? Yes
- Is Elder with me like you are in this existence? No
- When John sees shadow shapes, are they his guides? Yes and No
- Do you visit John as a shadow shape? Yes
- Has John spotted you as a shadow shape? Yes
- Are John's guides also appearing to him as shadow shapes? Yes and No
- Warick, are you also a spirit guide to John? Yes, and a slight No
- Are you mainly my spirit guide? Yes
- Are you one of John's spirit guides? Yes
- When you're not with me, are you with John? Yes

17 January 2021

Resumed journal entries

I know you're there now, Warick, slightly touching my right cheek. Increasingly, Warick is going quieter and quieter. Today, for the first time in probably over two years, I'm barely noticing him. Maybe six times in total through all different ways in the last twenty-four hours. I hate it! He might think he is doing the right thing giving me space now while so much is going on in my life. And a tiny feeling of him now on my right cheek. But from my perspective it's a load of bullshit! We are either in this team together—he and I—and do this thing together, or we don't. He is wrong. And if this is all he is now, and all he can do now, for whatever reason, he should go. They all should go. I feel lowest of the low. I feel abandoned again. If the *YouTube* sources on trance mediumship are right, where you need to say to Spirit, 'I give you my services' and completely give yourself over, just be a hollow pipe, well that's not for me and there are plenty of mediums out there, of which I'm not, who are really keen to become trance mediums, so please do me a favour and piss off! Take up shop somewhere else. I have the most incredible, bright and strong white light of a soul, and intelligence to go with it. WHY would I want to become a hollow pipe and not contribute anything that I am to a team effort??? Why is Warick letting me down now, because despite myself being completely willing, open and loving about whatever the future holds, I feel like I'm being pissed on right now! He is holding back, and I don't have any fucking idea why!!

20 January 2021

The United States has recorded 400,000 deaths, in the last year, as a result of COVID-19. I know Warick is with me because he just touched my right cheek, and I felt him in my face. In Donald Trump's farewell speech today, he said, 'This is just the beginning.' I have no words to say about all this right now. I feel numb. I'm sure if everyone in the world stopped in this moment and thought about their feelings, no one would have expected a year ago that all of this would happen one day. Today, a lady from the Unites States said in her interview that 'over 400,000 people have died so far from COVID-19, and it's like it doesn't matter'. She's right. When something starts to happen often enough—like terrorist attacks—it's like it suddenly becomes the norm. I feel numb. I'm sure I'll have more to say as I reflect on this under more normal circumstances, but not today. I'm going through a challenging time. Mum is selling up and moving in, and we are selling our investment property and refinancing and juggling our loans to buy the coastal house at Kianga. It means change for everyone. The main thing I want to say is how lucky I am that Mum and Ray are prepared to do this. It's my dream. For Ray, he loves our life in Yarralumla, Canberra. His heart and soul are there, and if he was the only person in the equation, I'm sure he wouldn't change a thing. He doesn't dislike the idea of having a place at the coast, but he doesn't like anything that threatens what he loves at Yarralumla. He is probably doing this mainly for me. For Mum, it's about her giving up where she has been happy and of course her living independence, which she is giving up probably a few years earlier than she would have liked. Once again, I think she's doing this because she knows it's my dream. She probably also doesn't like the idea of Ray and I being at Kianga while she is in Canberra. She likes somewhat the idea of coastal living, and she will be closer to my brother who lives only thirty minutes down the road. I don't think either of them would have done this if we didn't do it now. The strain on them both has been incredible. I haven't felt anywhere near as much strain as they have, probably because it's my dream and I think also because of the type of person I am. I don't mind change. I haven't been very happy for months because of the impact it's having on them, which I read as being very negative. Coinciding with this, I feel like Warick has stepped back from me, which of course I don't want to happen because of the joy he and spiritual engagement bring into my life. I love the continual diversity of what has happened over the last couple of years in particular. I've well and truly been having spirit experience withdrawal symptoms on top of what is happening on the home front.

Last night I listened to '432 Hz Healing Female Energy' by Power Thoughts Meditation and reflected on all the special moments during meditation with Warick, Elder, Wolf, Falcon, and Horse, as well as experiences with spirit energy in my physical life. Tears of love streamed down my cheeks. Warick was firmly in my face the whole time. I'm hoping he is only standing back because of what is happening in my personal life, but I don't know. I see the shadow shapes just as much as before. Through the night, Warick isn't waking me up, but if I do wake, he is there. He provides a gentle indication of his presence through a light vibration and some merging, as well as occasional very soft pulsing sounds. Nothing major. Maybe my vibrational frequency has dropped because I'm not as happy in myself. I may not be feeling and connecting as well. I don't know. The thought of Warick disappearing from my life and not progressing with my abilities to sense and interact with Spirit, is heartbreaking and distressing.

A couple of things worth noting from the last few days:

I had a dream where it was raining white feathers and drops of muddy water. I was walking along a path in a dry, hilly environment. The other night Warick spent quite a lot of time with me, moving around in my body and face. He also moved my head. Early the next morning, I also felt Warick in my throat area. The other night I watched a *YouTube* video on trance mediumship by Mark Bedwood where 'Charlie', a spirit he was channelling, said the medium's gatekeeper has a purple colour. I'm wondering if the purple I saw when I was at Jane's, was my gatekeeper or higher self, and the blue was Warick.

I've now sent the manuscript for the first *AWAKENING* journal to ten literary agents who are looking for work. One has already declined. Fingers crossed divine intervention comes into play, to help marry me up with the right agent. They need to be as passionate and enthusiastic as I am about all of this. They have an important role to play. I also want them there for the long haul.

Questions for Warick using the pendulum:

- Are you a spirit guide to all of us – John, Jules, Jane, and I? Yes
- Are you my main spirit guide? Yes
- Is Elder a spirit guide to Jules? No

Regarding the significance of the circle and triangles that you drew in Jane's lap:

- Did John connect us representing the corners of the two triangles joined at their peak? Yes
- Did Jane interpret correctly what you wanted by making the triangles and circle symbol in her lap? Yes
- Did I bring the circle together? Yes
- Is my symbol the circle? Yes
- Is John's symbol the triangle? Yes
- Is Jane's symbol the triangle? Yes

Note – Jules had already told me her symbol is a circle.

- Is each of our roles to help each other? Yes.
- Is Warick stepping away from me because of what is happening in my personal life? Yes
- Will you continue my development when things settle down? Yes
- Will you help me to connect to the right literary agent? Yes

22 January 2021

Resumed journal entries

A person now dies from COVID-19 in the United States every thirty-eight seconds. Yesterday, I watched Joe Biden become the forty-sixth president of the United States of America, and today I watched him sign their COVID-19 vaccine rollout plan where they want to vaccinate one hundred million people in their first one hundred days in office. Arnold Schwarzenegger, 'The Terminator', led the charge, encouraging others to join him in getting vaccinated. When I saw Joe Biden signing these important documents to help his nation and reverse the wrongs of Donald Trump, who didn't care about the rest of the world when he withdrew the United States contribution to the World Health Organisation, which made up twenty per cent of their funding, I thought to myself, 'I'm so glad you're in this job now. Don't let them down.'

My happiness level was up today, particularly this morning. Why? Because I had the most wonderful experience again with Warick last night. Given how things have been lately and how much I've missed new and evolving experiences with Warick, I wrote the following under mobile torch light at 2.15 this morning. I woke to localised pressure on my left and briefly saw what looked to be a small blue orb light above me moving to the left. It wasn't too bright. My body immediately got hot. I could feel Warick's energy merging with me all over, from head to toes. His energy pushed my facial features into what seemed to be his shape. I felt something extend from my external root chakra area which I have felt before. I'm wondering if it is Warick's penis. Never have I felt his energy in my throat as much as it was tonight. I experienced pressure and a tickle in my voice box. I heard him breathe through me, which I could tell because his breath is louder than mine. My eyes felt gritty. He moved my head up and extended my neck and head. I felt the sheet move above my left thigh, suggesting a physical change of me if his thighs are larger than mine. This went on for fifteen to twenty minutes and then it felt like he was gone. I find it interesting that although in his spiritual energy form he no longer has a body, he seems to use memory of his body to occupy mine. I'm physically being the body he had. It's fascinating. After this encounter with Warick, he made three pulse sounds. One had almost an electrical sound. It wasn't like his usual communication. It was like a surge of energy, which lasted about a second. It made me wonder if it was energy needing to be discharged after merging with a physical person. I remember Charlie, the spirit being channelled through Mark Bedwood on *YouTube*, said something about this.

This morning was lovely. Warick made me smile in response to some questions. I don't remember what, and he did three slow pulse sounds, which I interpreted as 'I Love You'. I'm happy.

26 January 2021

Australia Day. We've now spent twenty-four hours in our new home at Kianga on the coast of New South Wales. It feels very surreal. Warick is with me now. I feel him in my right cheek and forehead. He moves around a little. I love feeling him within me. It's just lovely. I'm completely comfortable with it and would miss him terribly if he no longer did this. Now I'm feeling a surge of heat, probably brought on by loving feelings towards Warick. My face perspires, glasses fog up, and I need to toss everything off. It took me quite some time to realise that these heat surges coincide with Warick engaging with me. I experienced perimenopause symptoms terribly a couple of years ago, but this has settled down. I can tell if they coincide with Warick or not, due to other spirit energy sensations I experience at the time.

    I'm having to make do with a notebook tonight. I'm sure I packed my journal, but do you think I can find it? No! I'm in my early fifties and have been physically treating my body as though I was twenty- or thirty-something lately. Thank God for all the personal training I've been doing the last couple of years. I feel stronger now than I did ten years ago. It's awesome! Anyway, I'm physically stuffed. All this moving and setting up our garden at Yarralumla to handle us not being there all the time to look after it. I moved two citrus trees to the coast: a bay leaf tree, Ray's father's rhubarb, two herbs, and two Star Jasmine plants. I also spread twelve bales of straw to make sure the Yarralumla garden would last a few weeks in the peak of summer before we return. The result has been my taking lots of painkillers. Now there is a garage full of boxes to empty. I'm glad I took the week off work.

    The night before last, Warick was there for me at Yarralumla. Ray had gone to Kianga early to do a pre-settlement inspection and collect house keys later that day. I gave up my bed for my brother who is eight years older than I and is suffering from a bad back. He has a plant freight business and brought one of his trucks to Canberra to move Mum and our plants to Kianga. Needless to say, my brother likes a few beers. Given he hasn't seen Mum for a long time, courtesy of the COVID virus, he was keen to sit up, sink a few, and chat with Mum. I, on the other hand, was exhausted and needed to go to bed, so I could get up at four in the morning to drive to the coast in time for the removalist arriving between eight and nine. I was in no mood for a late night. Given Ray took our spare foam mattress to Kianga to sleep on, I decided to buy a second foam mattress. Good decision. Even though I was on the dining room floor, it was pretty comfortable. I think Warick knew I was in a poor state because no sooner had I laid down and put my earphones in to listen to stormy weather and rain meditation sounds, he decided this wasn't the best choice. Even though I had the volume high and pressed the earphones into my ears, I could still hear my brother and Mum talking outside, which was incredibly annoying. Suddenly, some Google assistant kept prompting me to select music. I had no idea why. This has never happened before, and Warick just touched my right cheek agreeing with me. This must have happened at least four times. After a couple of times, I wondered if Warick was playing around with my phone. I closed *YouTube*, selected the meditation compilation I'd put together on Spotify and the problem was gone. It was very soothing and seemed louder than the meditation sounds on *YouTube*, so it effectively blocked out the sound of my brother and Mum talking. As I settled down, I felt Warick's energy in my face like he was letting me know he was there and comforting me. I fell asleep to one of the music tracks but then woke again about four hours later when I heard my brother come back downstairs searching for painkillers for his back. Then I heard Jamie moving about in his bedroom, which was above the room I was sleeping in. All in all, I had about four hours sleep before having to get up and get going. I left in the dark. I didn't feel like listening to blaring music, so I continued listening to the meditation music on Spotify while driving to the coast. It was lovely and I knew Warick was with me because I could feel his energy in my face on and off during the trip. Shortly after I started to descend the Clyde Mountain, just up ahead of me was our removalist hauling two shipping containers of our stuff. As I passed, I tooted at them and waved out the window, to which I received a loud and long blasting of their horn. I was happy because I knew I'd beat them to the house and would have time to see where Ray thought some of the furniture should go before they arrived. As I walked around with

Ray, I could see Warick as a shadow shape around me wanting to be a part of all the excitement. As usual, I acknowledged his presence in my mind. I said to Ray, 'Warick is here.' As usual, he rolled his eyes and brushed it off, not believing me. I think I have to stop making any comments about Warick at all. Ray doesn't believe it, nor is he interested. It deflates my elated feeling when he responds this way, so I think I need to keep it to myself. I find this sad to have to hide something so important to me and something that makes me feel so happy. Something I can't share or even talk about with Ray.

This morning was very special. As usual, I woke early in the morning before dawn to Warick being there. I could feel his vibration around the back left of my head and neck and also moving about in my face. I was still very tired so went back to sleep. It was a magic night because when I woke, I could hear the waves crashing on the beach. I didn't know if we were close enough to hear this, but we are, which is wonderful. I woke again about six in the morning. I felt pretty good and was too excited to stay in bed given I knew there was an amazing view of the coast and waves crashing on the beach on two sides of the house. I made a coffee and went out onto the front deck to watch it. This house is fantastic! It's situated high on the side of a hill overlooking the sea. It's two storeys high, with ocean views from almost every room, and it has large decks that wrap around the house, top and bottom. It's everything I dreamed of having one day, including a beautiful, professionally landscaped garden. I couldn't ask for more. I feel surreal and lucky. The person who built the house owned a ski resort. It was their holiday home. On my own, I sat on the upper deck and watched the sun rise over the ocean with a few clouds that made the colour amazing. It was very quiet. I felt Warick's energy solidly in my face, across my cheekbones, eyes and forehead. I'm sure he could see what I saw, through my eyes. When I asked him, he acknowledged it a couple of times by touching my right cheek. I talked with him about how beautiful it was as the sun rose and the lighting changed. We shared this first morning together, watching the sun rise over the ocean through the same eyes. It was very special.

28 January 2021

The night before last, Warick merged with me through the night. It's not like a complete merging where I no longer feel my physical body. This hasn't happened in a while. He seems to be focused on continuing to prepare me so he can speak through me, and a touch on the right cheek as I'm writing this suggests he agrees. I say he prepares me for speaking through me, because he has spent time in my throat, specifically my voice box. I've felt a slight pressure there, but also Warick has used it to make brief noises. Like what you do when you're clearing your throat if there is phlegm around the voice box. Yesterday, while unpacking boxes in the kitchen, several times I felt localised pressure in the air around me. I acknowledged its presence, said, 'Hi', and continued what I was doing.

Last night I was the last to go to bed. As I was walking across the living room floor, which I would say is in the middle of the house, I stopped to just take in the atmosphere of our new home. I stood in the dark with only the moonlight shining through the windows and hearing the waves crashing in the background. I experienced a very strong pressure in the air, on all sides of my body. I haven't experienced pressure like this before. It usually occurs on one side of my body and for a relatively short time. This time the pressure stayed. It was almost tangible. It was like filling the room with a dense foam and standing in the middle with it pushing in against your body. Amazing! I had no idea what it was. I'll have to see if it happens again and when I get a chance, also see if I can find something out about this type of experience online.

31 January 2021

Tonight, for the first time in over a week, things seem slightly—and I mean slightly—more peaceful. It's been such a tough week for Ray, Mum, Jamie, and me. From dawn until dusk, everyday unpacking boxes. There were over one hundred! Mostly Mum's stuff, as all her things have been moved to the coast. It certainly is testing our relationships at the moment. Anyway, something I'm really noticing this last week is I'm feeling Warick strongly as localised pressure changes around me. I don't know if it is only Warick, but I think it is. It feels like my ear is experiencing a pressure change, like when you descend from a mountain or an airplane. All week, on and off through the day, this localised pressure has been following me around the house.

Last night was amazing. I was sound asleep facing the centre of the bed, then something—a presence on the side of the bed next to me— woke me. I turned to face that direction and immediately felt a strong pressure in a large space on the side of the bed. I was half asleep, but thought it was Warick, so I said in my mind, 'Hi Warick. Do you want to merge with me?' He started to do so immediately. He merged with my entire body. Not to the point where I couldn't feel my body anymore, but it was strong. This went on for what seemed like at least a couple of hours. A couple of times his energy seemed to go quiet, but as soon as I reached out mentally, Warick was there again merging with me. He certainly is close to me at the moment, day and night, which I love, but I also appreciate it very much given the stresses and what feels like unhappiness stemming from Mum and Ray. I hope things settle down and I hope they will be happy here. I love it. I wish I could share that excitement with someone. The sadness and strain this week have also been rubbing off on Jamie. It's not a good time.

1 February 2021

A technician came this morning to connect the house at Kianga to the internet. He and I moved around the house to test the network capacity in each room. When we went into the second bedroom upstairs, which is where I plan to work and use as a guest bedroom, I entered first. As soon as I moved into the room, I felt a significant presence in the air to the left side of the room. I also saw shadow shapes moving about in the room. They were really distinct, and larger than what I often associate with Warick. I love it when I sense and feel spirit energy. It's very special as I'm literally sensing another form of existence that most people don't experience. I feel so very lucky. I just wish I could communicate with them so I can understand if they sense me and are trying to get my attention. What do they want to tell me? This makes me think of how John holds a casual conversation with Spirit using the Panabox. I acknowledge spirit energy and let them know I appreciate them being there. Every now and then, I wonder where, if anywhere, this is all leading to. Am I making the most of this unique and wonderful opportunity? Could I be doing more to help things evolve? I'm feeling Warick touch the right side of my cheek now, and again, and now for a third time. This suggests I could be doing a lot more to help things along. I wish I knew the bits I'm not getting right or could do more of. I feel exhausted at the moment, with the big move to the coast, so it's not a good time to start beating myself up over another thing.

3 February 2021

This evening is the first time Ray and I have taken the dogs to the beach for a walk. The dogs have never seen the ocean before. Rosie, a little Choodle, loved it. She was elated in her doginality, and Max, the Jack Russell, also enjoyed it. They are getting on in age, both eleven years old. One has Cushing's disease, and the other has Addison's disease. Both are dependent on medicine daily. I hope they love their final years here, with the occasional trip to Canberra, their original home. What was really noticeable and just lovely, was as soon as I got on the beach, I saw Warick's shadow shape around me wanting to be part of this first important experience for the dogs. I kept seeing his shadow shape getting my attention everywhere I looked. It was just terrific! In my mind, of course I kept acknowledging him. I hope he picked up on my communication with him.

13 February 2021

Alaiza's birthday today. I must remember to send her birthday wishes. When Jamie spent ten days with us moving and unpacking, Alaiza called with wonderful news. Her Australian permanent residency application was approved. It was surprising news because we thought she was going to be granted a visa to stay in Australia based on her de facto relationship with Jamie. Instead, her application was taken straight through to permanent residency, and she got the news on Australia Day. I was absolutely over the moon. My voice octave jumped a few bars higher, and I was almost squealing when Jamie told us. We had to call her straight away to say congratulations. I really admire Alaiza; she has done it all on her own to make a start in this country, with no help. It's been tough and she has hung in there. I couldn't be happier.

While I think about it, I'll describe an experience that happened last night and then step back in time to talk about a couple of others. Warick is touching my right cheek, just gently, letting me know he's here. I'm sure Warick is working towards being able to talk through me. Several sources, including the Seth Series, Mark Bedwood's *YouTube* videos, Jane Hall and Phil Dykes, and Kerry McLeod from My Mediumship in the United Kingdom, suggest it takes a long time for Spirit to be able to talk through a person. It can take years. I know why. Because it's a very gradual process. I can only speak from my own experience, but for me it's getting used to the feeling of Warick's energy moving my face, head and body. I think he will also control my breathing because I've noticed like last night, I experience one or two involuntary quick breaths when I'm starting to drift off to sleep. I'm getting a light touch from Warick on my right cheek now, so I gather this is right. I think he is also starting to get me used to him moving my conscious mind aside, so I'm not conscious of what he is doing. Each time this happens, I'm not expecting it, and I quickly jolt back when I realise what's happening. When I noticed I wasn't really relaxing, I kept saying to myself, 'Relax, relax, relax.' That seemed to help a bit. It's an interesting process. I'll keep writing about it as I notice different things and stages of progress.

Over three successive nights this last week, I've had the most terrible thing happen. My feet and calf muscles of both legs have simultaneously been clenching and cramping. I also felt pins and needles around my feet, my calves and up to my knees. It was really horrible. I couldn't sleep. Each night this went on until I'd get up and rub Voltaren gel into my calves and feet and take a couple of painkillers. I've never experienced anything like it. It was really bad. I said to Ray if it keeps it up, I'll have to go to a doctor to see what's wrong. The next night, it stopped completely. I now get the usual tingling around my feet that I associate with connecting with Warick or another dimension, but nothing like what happened those few nights. I'm making a record of this in case it ends up being connected to something significant. Just after this experience occurred, I found out my sister had a fall in the night and cracked her vertebrae—three actually—and was flown to Sydney to be operated on by a neurosurgeon. I'm yet to hear what the consequences are going to be. I suspect my feet and legs experience is not related, but we shall see what her symptoms are going to be longer term. Hopefully she will recover really well.

The other morning, while washing my hair in the shower, I noticed the familiar two dots connected by a line floating past about ten centimetres from my chest. Seeing shadow shapes in the shower is not uncommon for me but I had to write about it because there it was, very clear, just happily floating past me, like it was business as usual. I have a very interesting existence with Spirit. It sometimes just makes me smile.

The last thing I wanted to mention is I cancelled the circle session tomorrow with John, Jules and Jane. After the last few stressful weeks, which ended with a horrible two weeks of work with no breaks, I feel completely exhausted and run down. I tried to consult with Warick ahead of time, but he wouldn't give me his opinion, so I assumed it was up to me. I hope to reschedule for a month's time.

The very last thing I want to mention is I've noticed that when I message John now, just like when I'm writing in this journal, Warick has started to show up, interested in what I'm writing. It's probably because he knows I'm writing about spirit engagement. It's really nice because it's like Warick is saying hi to John. Just lovely.

14 February 2021

Valentine's Day! My heart wasn't in it this year. Ray had a week in Canberra, recuperating from the big move in solitude. He made an effort. I didn't. A beautiful blush pink satin bathrobe and a beautiful card with personal reflections. A flower decorated box with a lovely black evening dress and necklace and earrings to match. I had done nothing. No doubt the last few months have been the worst time in our relationship. I've been gradually drifting away for years. That said, I value and love Ray very much. I will never let him down in this lifetime. I do enjoy his company but not all the time. That's fine, because nobody is perfect, and I know I'm complex and definitely difficult to be around at times. Lately, I have loved him a little. It's very difficult when up until recently your partner has gone in the same direction, but now my heart is in Kianga and Ray's is in Yarralumla. I've had to extract myself, and I'm still doing so to be here. To try to be closer to who I am. One day, I hope to be able to spend most of my time just being who I am, rather than being all I can be for others. The part that is me is silent. It's all inside. No wonder I'm close to Spirit. They are the only ones who know what I think and engage me on what I'm interested in with spirit and nature.

Tonight, I want to write about two things. The other night, I had a dream about John for the first time. It went on for quite some time. I've been to'ing and fro'ing about whether to let him know. I think I will. I'm always treading on eggshells when it comes to John's consciousness. I think quite rightly, it serves him very well. The way I think about John is like when you had a time in your life, particularly as a child, with a close friend, just lying in a field, staring at the sky, and feeling completely at ease and peace with each other. You know each other is there, but you don't feel like you need to say something, unless a thought comes to mind that you want to share. The other responds in a way that is at ease like you are. I'm like this when I garden with my mother. It's been like this my entire life. Just two souls tending the garden together, usually apart, busily doing something, but within hearing distance. This was my dream with John the other night. Head to head and bodies lying in opposite directions, in a field looking at the sky and talking to each other when thoughts came to mind. Perfectly at ease. Nothing to do with physical life. Just two souls in each other's company. It was lovely.

The other thing I want to write about is actually two things. This morning when I awoke, it was magic. The moment I started to wake, Warick was already merged with me and he took control of my mouth and made it smile. It was lovely. This naturally moved on to Warick opening my mouth of his own accord, and quite wide, and feeling my throat muscles constrict as though it was going to be used to speak. He was showing me what he could do now, and I feel Warick on my right cheek as I'm writing this, agreeing with my recollections. I praised him in my mind, saying how clever he is. Incredibly special, and another significant step towards his being able to speak through me.

Tonight, Ray is in Canberra, and Mum and my brother are downstairs asleep at Kianga. While getting a few things out of my bag I'd taken to Canberra, I pulled out two beautiful metal candelabra that I'd bought before meeting Ray, to put on our new dining table. I thought they would suit our new table as it's long, made with pieces of recycled wood on the top. It reminds me of something you'd see in a dining hall in a castle. The room has a vaulted ceiling, with a very long wall on one side. It certainly has the *feeling* of a dining hall in a castle. As I was placing them on the table in the dark, I felt the pressure that I've been feeling since arriving. It was around my arms and shoulders. I decided to pause, acknowledge its presence, and talk to it. I talked about how special this place is, how much I love it and would look after it. I kept feeling a touch on a finger on my left hand while I was still touching one of the candelabra on the table. I know the spirit knew I was talking to it and understood what I was saying. It was responding by touching my fingers. I said I hoped it would stay and how I liked its presence. I hope it does stay if it wants to. Or comes and goes if it chooses.

When I cancelled the circle, I asked John, Jules and Jane if they knew if when a new owner moves into a house, spirits sometimes come back so they can check them out. I'm sure this happened with Patricia in Yarralumla when Jamie and I sensed her when we first moved in, and now in our new house at Kianga. Jane responded saying you can often feel spirit presences when you first move into a new place.

18 February 2021

Free handwriting questions and answers with Warick.
Note – during this session I felt Warick firmly in my face and when responding to some questions he moved my head of his own accord.

- It's been a long time Warick, since using this means to communicate. Yes
- Is it Warick who is still with me? Yes
- Will things continue to progress with me? Yes
- Are you drifting away? No
- Will our book *AWAKENING* get published? Yes, and Warick made my head nod.
- Are you and I meant to record our experiences together and have them published as books? Yes, and Warick made my head nod.
- Have I missed this opportunity to connect and evolve with Spirit? No
- What is your purpose being with me? Love
- What is the one bit of advice you'd like to give me now? Patience
- Is this right? (I was checking if I interpreted his written answer correctly) Yes
- Is the spirit world helping to get our book published? Yes
- Will one of the literary agents I've sent it to so far, want to publish it? Yes
- Will I hear from them soon? Yes
- Do you want to talk through me? Yes
- Will you try that soon? Yes
- Will sitting in a circle with John, Jules and Jane help you talk through me? Yes

28 February 2021

Resumed journal entries

Hi Warick. I feel you in my cheeks, eyes and forehead. Nice of you to join me. When I woke last night and turned the clock to read the time, which said it was three in the morning, I immediately thought, 'This is a good sign.' That time seems to have significance for many who experience Spirit, as it's this time when supposedly the veil between our dimensions is at its thinnest, enabling spirits to come through. I tend to think it's when most people are in an ideal relaxed state, which enables them to sense Spirit. It's when your conscious mind is resting, which enables your subconscious to experience Spirit. Warick is just touching my right check twice, so I suspect I have this interpretation partly or wholly correct.

I have not been writing in the journal often lately. I'd have to say it's been one of the hardest times in my life. Not the packing, moving, unpacking, fixing things, getting things the way we like them, and getting into a routine of living between the coast and Canberra, but rather it's the reaction and negativity from Mum, Ray and me. It's been really bad. There have been quite a few unexpected things pile on top of this, like my sister breaking her back, tiles sliding down the roof at Yarralumla, leaving a gaping hole, the modem blowing up due to a lightning strike, and discovering the Kianga house roof leaks, which has affected three rooms. I understand Mum's behaviour as she is eighty-three; however, Ray, who has managed to cope with a very stressful job for thirty years, whereby it's in its very nature where the unexpected happens a lot, has not coped with events of the last few months. So much so, it's got to a point where I can see there is less drama if I do things myself, like arranging tradesmen to fix things. I feel like I can't ask him to do anything. When unexpected things happen when I'm working, and my job is also being very demanding, I find it a lot to cope with. It exhausts me and I find I don't have much left in me for others. I wish Ray would take things in his stride and be easier going, but for some reason he's not. He certainly isn't the person he used to be, nor does he treat me with respect. This is not a good time for us and certainly is straining our relationship.

Recently, John said some lovely wise words knowing the difficult time I'm going through. He has complete trust that the circumstances will change for the better. He said it always does.

Last night, once again when I noticed it was 3.00 am on the clock, I thought this was a good sign. Warick is with me every day and night. I love him being there. I do miss the diversity of things I experienced with him and hope they return. He is touching my right cheek now, I guess saying, 'Yes, it will.' That said, he has been working on my voice box at times during the night. While in a semi-asleep state it took me a while to realise what he was doing. I don't usually snore but when I do, I usually wake myself up with the sound. Initially, I just thought I was starting to snore, and then I woke enough to realise the sound was coming from my throat, specifically my voice box. Just a short little noise, like when you want to discreetly clear your throat. I also realised I wasn't initiating the sound, Warick was. Sometimes he would do this half a dozen times, leave it, and then do it again, all while I was awake and consciously aware of what he was doing. Really interesting.

With all the negativity in the house, John suggested saging/smudging the house. I've never done this before, and the more I go on the less inclined I am to feel I need any tools to engage with Spirit. That said, yesterday I stopped and bought two sage sticks from what John calls a metaphysical shop from a small village just south of Batemans Bay. It is called Mogo and is on the way to Kianga. Mum is intrigued and keen to be a part of the process to hopefully clear any negative energy from the house. Ray is in Canberra this week so it's a good time to do it. After Mum had gone to bed, I turned all the lights out and sat on my exercise mat in the middle of the house, where I had felt the pressure all around me shortly after we moved in. In my mind, I spoke to the house, wanting to detect any negative energy and to ask it to leave. Three times I experienced this incredible rush of energy. It literally was like I was in a wind tunnel, with the wind rushing fiercely past my entire body, but it wasn't wind it was energy. It felt like a vacuum, and I couldn't hear anything else. The rush of energy lasted at least thirty seconds each time. It wasn't coming from any particular direction, but I did feel it rushing through me. Each time I said to myself over and over again, 'With love and light.' Eventually, the energy rush subsided. It was incredible! I've never experienced anything like it. It didn't feel threatening or negative. It was just absolutely full on. I honestly don't know what it was. Mum and I will sage the house today.

Although I haven't been writing in the journal, I have been keeping a note of a few things when they happened. While working on 19 February, there was an instant jump to high volume on the speaker as I was playing music. It didn't happen again and hasn't happened before with this speaker. I assumed it was Warick, or a spirit around me either trying to get my attention or show me what it can do. One night, while lying in bed, pressure came forward in my face uniformly. It just arrived without feeling it come into my body and spread through my face, which is what usually happens. Warick has led me to a few relevant things while reading the Seth series. I've been curious about the pressure I've been experiencing here at Kianga, and how it has been noticeably different to what I experience in Canberra. In the book, Seth said, 'Atmospheric conditions are more right for his coming through for a session with Jane.' It made me wonder about being close to the ocean and surf beach, which is full of constantly moving energy. It's possible this is enabling Warick to come through more strongly, assuming the pressure is Warick, which I don't know if it is. It was also interesting to learn recently, that Jane's husband uses the pendulum to validate things for himself, like I do. On 19 February while reading the Seth series, Seth talked about integrating his personality with Jane's, and how it enables her to have a greater ability to use intuition and knowledge. I think his reference to knowledge means the ability of a medium to just know things through claircognizance. On 21 February, while reading the Seth series in the middle of the night, Seth talked about how a person can pick up the physical symptoms of others sympathetically. You need to ground yourself, clear the mind and suggest that all alien impulses and conditions be removed. I do wonder if this explains the bad back that I had when Mum was moving, where I shared the same symptoms in the same part of the body that she did. I also wonder if my feeling down lately is because I've been taking on Ray's and Mum's negativity. Somehow, I need to protect myself from this occurring.

On 23 February, I used the pendulum to ask Warick a few questions. Immediately, Warick started to respond by touching my cheeks, so in the end I didn't bother with the pendulum.

- Will this difficult time pass? Yes
- Is John still keen to be my friend? Yes
- Are you disappointed in me? Yes. Warick agrees I'm letting everyone down.
- Will you keep developing me to sense and experience Spirit? Yes
- Will you and John's guides keep developing our ability to collectively sense Spirit? Yes
- Will you speak through me one day? Yes

On 24 February, while in the bathroom doing my hair before going out for dinner, pressure arrived on the left side of my head and stayed there for at least five minutes. I reached out mentally and spoke to it, encouraging engagement and to provide me with a sign, but I got nothing. Reflecting on the first morning back in Canberra, when two tiles slid down the roof, leaving a large hole, and two mornings later when a lightning strike blew up our internet modem, it made me wonder if bad energy was following me around. I wondered if the Yarralumla house was not happy because we are no longer there all the time. I noticed several times when Ray and I have been away for six weeks or so overseas, that when we return, something immediately stops working and we need to get it fixed. It's like the house—or spirits in the house—are acting out or wanting our attention. It's happened several times before, where I've previously wondered if this is what had been happening.

3 March 2021

Every morning when I wake, I see the most beautiful views of the ocean. Here I am sitting in bed. It's early morning with the sun rising, and I'm looking straight out to the horizon over the ocean. It's amazing! The ocean is constantly changing from flat and calm to choppy seas and crashing waves. I absolutely love it. It's wild. Nothing can control it—even humans. I feel like I'm co-existing with this massive beast alongside our home. Its mood affects what we can do. We live up high with incredible views. It's a very exposed area. Our house experiences the full fury of winds when there is a gale blowing. It's still very early days but Mum and I are starting to bond with the garden and have undertaken some pretty major projects already. Mum is just like a gnome in the garden, pottering around and tending to the plants. Often the only way to find her is at the end of the garden hose. It will be interesting to see what happens with Ray, whose heart is in Yarralumla, Canberra. Many of his friends retired recently so he enjoys spending time with them. It will be interesting to see if he ends up spending most of his time in Canberra. I'm spending most of my time at Kianga with trips to work in Canberra every second week. I'd love to be retired from the kind of work I do and instead focus on Spirit and writing about these experiences. This is what I love now. It's where my passion and curiosity lie. Given the negativity in the house of late, I took up John's suggestion and saged the house with Mum on the weekend. She and I sat facing each other in the centre of the house, quietening our minds. I immediately felt Warick touch my cheek to let me know he was there, and a while later when I asked Mum if she felt anything she said she experienced a brush against her right leg. All the windows were open, and while moving from room to room, I brushed smoke in all directions talking to whatever may be there. I said, 'Energy of good intention is welcome to stay and that which isn't, must leave'. I said, 'We come with love and light.'

I also said, 'Our negative energy of late is not who we are, and we have no bad intentions.' The energy throughout the house seemed to be uniform. I felt no pressure or anything else. In a subsequent email, John said I need to open every cupboard and all drawers, so I may do it again one day to be sure. That all said, I tend to think this is an old tradition, ritualistic and using tools, which I'm not into. I prefer to sit quietly, reach out with my senses, and communicate with my mind to whatever is in my presence. I'll do this again soon. I enjoy it. I had another really interesting dream with John in it the other night. It was the first time I met him in person. We arranged to meet at a hotel where I think we were staying. He had a male friend with him who was also into Spirit. I think we were meeting up to experiment moving between dimensions. His friend seemed nice, and we spent quite a lot of time together. There was an awkwardness, however, between me and John. Like we were avoiding each other to some extent. Maybe it's because in real life we are comfortable with our virtual engagement. We have never spoken to each other.

4 March 2021

Yesterday morning was like Armageddon in the house at Kianga. All three smoke alarms were sounding off like they were talking to each other. There was no timing or pattern to it. At times, there were many instances of beeps, then a quiet period, and then beeping again. Max, our Jack Russell, particularly dislikes high pitch beeping sounds, so the dogs weren't happy either. I couldn't work out how to disconnect one of the smoke alarms. Luckily, a man showed up, who visited with carpet samples and was measuring up the bedrooms. He managed to help take down two of the smoke alarms, with the third we discovered was hard wired in. I took out the battery from the one I thought needed to be replaced. Being concerned about missing time at work, I went down to ask Mum if she wouldn't mind going out to get new batteries. Still in her dressing gown and eating her breakfast, she agreed. I felt bad asking given her sleepy state. While I was asking Mum, out the corner of my eye, I saw a small brown dog with a big grin on its face merrily trotting up to her front sliding door. Of course, our dogs got set off and were barking at it. I've never seen the dog before. It looked quite old. Next minute, with smoke alarms still sounding off, even though I took the battery out of one of them, Rosie seemed to have disappeared. I found her out the front of the house, suggesting she had found a hole in the fence and got out. I suppose she was interested in the brown dog that had shown up. I found a gap under the side picket fence so plugged it with a brick, thinking this is where she had escaped. As Mum was leaving to get batteries, I noticed Rosie was out the front again. This time I stood on one side of the fence and called her, hoping she would show me where she got out. She obligingly pushed a paling in the fence where there were no nails. While Mum was out, I found some nails in the garage, which were a bit short, and used them to hold the paling in place. In the meantime, I was trying to log on to the computer to get work started for the day. The fire alarms were still sounding off on a regular basis. When Mum returned, I mentioned the nails were too short to which she said she would go out again to get some longer ones. The house was in chaos! I was late for two teleconference meetings. Feeling desperate, in the second meeting I asked if anyone knew anything about fire alarms to which a bunch of IT guys were not much help. By lunchtime, I had changed the batteries twice with no success in fixing the problem, so I pulled the batteries out and left the units sitting on the breakfast bar. No luck. Once again smoke alarm sounds kept beeping with no particular pattern or timing. I assumed the one causing all the trouble was the one that was hard wired downstairs. I had a quick lunch, realising how disrupted my workday had been so far, and then looked up electricians at Narooma. Someone from one of the companies felt sorry for me, so they arranged for someone to come first thing the next morning (today) to see what the problem was. Last night, the alarm continued to beep every hour, so I used ear plugs to get some sleep.

Yesterday was absolutely crazy. Last night after work I had a stiff double Scotch on ice and tried to laugh about it. I don't know how many times I carried the ladder from the garage upstairs to dismantle the smoke alarms. I lost count. Mum said Rosie wasn't herself all day. I could see this too. Rosie is highly perceptive. When Mum went to bed, I put Max to bed and decided to sit in the middle of the living room with Rosie to see what I could feel and maybe have a good talking to whatever may have had a hand in the day's events. Rosie wriggled on and off as I was having this conversation, like she wasn't completely comfortable being there. Once again, I felt this wave of energy come over me that feels like a vacuum. And it stayed there, completely consuming me for a minute or so. I concentrated on my feelings of good intentions, determined not to let it rattle me. It's not a bad experience, as I've said before, but it is very distinct. I don't think it's Warick. During the night, Warick woke me a couple of times with his vibration, which was nice, and he was keen to progress practising using my voice box. I asked if he wanted me to say a few words to get things going, which is something Jules said she does when she starts to channel Spirit. I said probably three words and kept my mouth slightly open. As my mind started to wander, Warick made a brief sound with my voice box, like clearing my throat with a 'ca' sound. He would have done this at least ten times, and each time it coincided with me becoming more relaxed when my mind started to wander off. It was really cool.

5 March 2021

2.25 am. One of the good things about Ray being away is that I can turn on the light in the middle of the night and start writing in my journal. A short while ago, Warick woke me when moving his energy into my face where I thought he would do some work with my voice box. Instead, his engagement seemed to stop, and I experienced a high pitch tone a couple of times in my left ear. It was nice. It was a higher pitch than what I've experienced at other times. I acknowledged that a spirit was trying to communicate with me. Then I sensed pressure around me. Not strong, just subtle. I felt localised, cool air move around my legs and bottom and wondered if it was Warick. I don't think so. Then I felt little tickles on my right cheek. I wish I could communicate with these spirits that visit me. I hope they know I recognise they are there.

It was a peaceful day in the house today compared with the smoke alarm saga yesterday. As promised, two electricians came early in the morning and replaced all three units. I've been struggling to get my balance back since we moved to Kianga. I'm now managing to exercise most weekdays but only one type of exercise each day. Walking or strength training. I need to do both as each have their benefits in different ways. When I walk here at Kianga, a round trip of six kilometres gets me to Duesbury Beach and back. I walk past my favourite beach, 'Kianga Beach', and the next along the road is Duesbury Beach. It's a lovely little beach. Just like Kianga Beach, it has great waves. It has a small headland with a lookout on top. That's my halfway point where I stop for a few minutes to look down at the waves crashing onto the beach and the rocks. It's absolutely beautiful. Each time I've stopped there I've felt Warick move into my face. I can feel him looking through my eyes. I've confirmed this with him several times now. I hope this brings him some happiness. It's the least I can do for him. It's very special, sharing moments like these.

Yesterday, John sent me a preview of his latest paranormal investigation video. It was terrific! Really professionally done, with a wonderful combination of history, interviews and investigation. It was at a place called Odd Fellows Hall in Vancouver, Canada. Odd Fellows was a society that spread across many countries believing in the betterment of humanity. Their motto was 'Friendship, Love and Truth'. They seemed to do many positive things. Anyway, John used a combination of devices to detect movement and sound. A Panabox, which he invented, was used to detect voices. He also used a historian and a medium and held interviews with a few Odd Fellow members who have spent many years in the building. He detected a really good range of instances of Spirit. I particularly liked it when John was videoing himself talking in the car outside the building, where a few spirit orbs moved around him. It was beautiful. They were obviously curious about John and what he was doing.

I've been reading some interesting material by Seth on his explanation about reincarnation. He said the inner self is composed of all the potential egos that compose it. He said they are the result of psychological experience gained in past lives. These egos at one time or another have had their chance at being the dominant ego in this existence or in another incarnation. Just as I'm writing now, a very subtle pressure energy has moved slowly around my head, popping in to see what I'm doing. As usual, I have now become very hot, having to toss off the bed clothes. I often get hot when Warick, and possibly another spirit is around me. Seth says that reincarnation does not imply a reoccurring time system. He said reincarnation needs to be considered in the context of the spacious present. He said the separate existences occur simultaneously. Past, present and future all exist now. You exist in several incarnations at one time in the spacious present. You are forming past, present and future experiences simultaneously. The whole self, or identity, is aware of the experiences of all the egos, and since one identity forms these egos there is bound to be similarities in characteristics between them. Something else Seth said that I'm trying to get my head around is the physical body itself is never the same. The atoms that compose it, appear and disappear constantly, where the appearance of permanency is retained. He claims the personalities can alternate as the body changes. I look forward to when I retire and have time to reread much of the Seth series. There are some really interesting concepts to think about, some of which may help to explain some of the things I've experienced.

8 March 2021

I've just had the most amazing couple of days. The sagas at Kianga have continued with my coming within half a metre of a 1.5 metre red-bellied black snake in our backyard. I was carrying a tray of pansy seedlings, about to head up the steps next to a three-tiered rockery garden that I had recently cleared of agapanthus. Our encounter was a shock to both of us. Given our close proximity, my immediate concern was if it would chase me. It was big and way too close for my liking. The snake made a beeline straight up the rockery garden and into a hole, just like it knew exactly where it was going. At the same time, I was slowly stepping away in the opposite direction. It was a Sunday afternoon so not easy to get in touch with someone to remove it. I remembered my nephew had done a snake handling course for his job working for national parks. He sent me a few numbers to call, which led me to a guy who generously spent considerable time on the phone telling me all about the snake's likely habitat, time of year and behaviours. There was no point in his coming unless he could get to the snake, which we assumed wouldn't be possible as it had disappeared into a hole. After the call, Mum insisted on my showing her the hole the snake went in. I'm glad she did, because when I took a closer look, I could see the snake in the hole. I was straight back on the phone to the guy who said he was on his way. He told me to guard the hole and said if the snake knew I was there, it wouldn't come out. I decided to play music on my phone near the hole as I didn't think I'd be able to keep talking for the time it would take for the guy to drive to our house. Within about ten minutes of the guy arriving, he managed to aggravate the snake enough with a hook wire that it came out and started to take off across the lawn, heading for the agapanthus on the fence line. The guy followed it quickly, and after a couple of tries he managed to pick it up by the tail. It was long, confirming the estimated 1.5

metres I thought it was. We were so relieved to see the snake go headfirst into the guy's bag. The snake would have to be relocated a few kilometres away to make sure it didn't return.

The night before last was incredible. I may have mentioned a few entries ago that I had this dream where I met up with John and his friend at a hotel where we were staying. It was nighttime and we were experimenting with the ability to access different dimensions. I don't remember the approach we were taking. Anyway, the night before last when I couldn't sleep, I started to read the Seth series again. Warick's energy was firmly in my face, and he assumed reading along with me. I came across two sections in Session 260 that blew me away. The first was Seth encouraging Jane and her husband to try and meet up with each other in dreams. The second talked about 'mental or psychic journeys into other dimensions and systems being possible'. Seth said that mentally you can cut through space whereas physically you can't. In some of your dream states, you can travel through other dimensions and other systems. It was incredible, because as usual Warick led me to read something shortly after I'd been curious about it. I had been curious about the dream and had messaged John about it. It's almost like the dream with John was about meeting up in our dreams like Seth had suggested to Jane and her husband, and in our case to experiment travelling to other dimensions. I don't think it was a premonition where the dream happened, and soon after I read about the same type of thing. It's more like Warick was telling me the dream I had was intentional. It's possible he wants me to think about meeting up with John in the dream state for the purpose of trying to access other dimensions. Incredible!

Last night, Warick merged with my entire body. I suspect Warick is in a male form because on several occasions I feel what I think are his genitals extended down between my legs outside of my root chakra. It's very distinct, as is the way my head moves. I'm sure I'm taking on his form.

17 March 2021

Questions for Warick with touches on my cheek responses:

- Will you and other spirit guides help to line up a publisher for the first book, *AWAKENING*? Yes
- Do I need to send the manuscript to more publishers? Yes
- Will I send it to the publishers who will be interested? Yes
- Warick, were you at John's place and turned up his TV loud before he got home? Yes
- Are you a guide for John? Yes
- Are you John's main guide? No
- Does John suspect you are one of his guides? Yes
- Is it because he experiences similar things to me? Yes
- Did you agree to be a guide to both of us? No response
- Will you and other spirits give me a sign that you're going to help get my book published? Yes
- Will I continue as a contractor for years to come? Yes
- Do you think I write well? No, then Yes
- Will I become a recognised writer to get this information to the world? Yes
- Will it happen in this physical lifetime? Yes
- Will it be what I do when I retire? No
- Will I achieve this before I retire? Yes
- In this round of submitting the manuscript, will a publisher say they want to work with me? No, then Yes, then Yes

18 March 2021

Resumed journal entries

I feel Warick in my face now, joining me for this journal entry. I've noticed lately when I'm driving my car between Canberra and Kianga that I can feel Warick in my face—around my eyes in particular. It's an incredibly scenic drive, and I think Warick can see through my eyes when I feel his presence in this area of my face. I hope he's enjoying the drive but doesn't have plans to one day drive the car through me. When I can feel him in my face as I'm driving, I sometimes joke with him saying, 'I don't think you would be a very good driver.'

The dramas at home have continued with Max picking up a paralysis tick in his mouth from the garden. This must have happened around the same time the snake showed up because only a couple of days later, after having travelled to Canberra with the dogs, Max was behaving unusually. He was scratching at his mouth, which he sometimes does, then he was coughing and gagging one morning. He sometimes looked at me with a very sad look, and one evening he made a little high-pitched whine as though something was wrong. I talked to Ray about taking him to the vet and booked an appointment on the Saturday when we would be back in Kianga. He didn't last that long. By Friday afternoon, when he returned from a walk with Ray, he was starting to lose his balance in his back legs. I said to Ray, 'He needs help now.' We then packed up Max in the car and took him to the emergency veterinary hospital in Canberra. The person on the counter immediately suspected a tick and asked if we had been to the coast recently. They took Max straight through to be examined, located the tick in his mouth, then had him on a drip with anti-venom. They graded him as about halfway gone by way of paralysis symptoms. It was 'touch and go' for the next twenty-four hours as to whether he would survive. Thankfully, he did, and we collected him on Sunday afternoon. Since then, I've been babying him as the effects of the paralysis venom won't wear off for a couple of weeks. He tries to bark but has no voice.

An interesting coincidence occurred on 12 March. Before I realised I had to take Max to the emergency vet hospital, John sent me a series of *YouTube* videos about a woman who psychically communicates with animals. Her name is Anna Breytenbach. Her abilities are incredible. John was urging me to watch them as they resonated with him. Looking back, I wonder if Warick had used John to give me a sign that I needed to try and understand what Max was telling me. I also wonder if the snake encounter was a sign, because like the tick, it is also venomous and dangerous. When I arrived in Canberra, and before taking Max to the vet, I also saw lots of white feathers on the front steps of our porch. I didn't pay too much attention because it's quite common to see feathers around our house in Canberra. This is because there is a colony of cockatoos that fly over in the morning and at dusk. I also came across a grey feather on our front steps, which is not common—possibly belonging to a pigeon. I kept this one and later researched on *YouTube* the significance of feathers. It said white feathers are a sign your angels are with you and trying to give you a message. Interestingly, grey feathers are a sign you need to bring balance back into your life. This, I know, at the moment, is very true, and has been bothering me. I still haven't managed to find time to exercise regularly and eat well.

22 March 2021

Thanks, Warick, for letting me know you're there by touching my right cheek as I start to write. Right now, in this house, it feels like the calm before the storm. Since I've been back at Kianga the last few days, it's been raining. There has been significant flooding on the northern New South Wales coast, and tomorrow, three hundred schools will be closed. Tomorrow, the weather bureau predicts will be our worst day with severe weather warnings, gale winds and flooding in neighbouring townships, with one hundred per cent rain predicted every hour all day. Right now, there is silence. No rain. No wind. And the temperature is mild. The calm before the storm.

We still have at least four leaks in our ceiling in the living room. I have a routine going—cycling towels on the floor below the leaky spots, then hanging those not being used over the balustrade on the stairwell going down to Mum's flat. In myself, I'm feeling better. John has sent encouraging words and good advice. I also came across a woman on *YouTube* called BK Shivani, who had a perfect video on how to protect yourself from negative energy being displaced by other people. I highly recommend watching it. It's terrific! It's called 'Protect yourself from people's emotions: Part 2: BK Shivani'. She says there are three choices when someone is being negative towards you. You can (1) reflect the negative emotion back at someone, which just perpetuates the negative energy; (2) absorb the negative energy, which in turn makes you feel negative; or (3) transform the negative energy by understanding the person being negative is not right in themselves. She encourages you to try and transform the way they feel, but also through understanding them, you protect yourself from becoming negative. I'm sure this is what I've been doing with Ray and Mum—absorbing and reflecting their negative energy. My usual happy self has become tired and stressed, so my usual protection 'positivity' is very down. I need to go back to seeking to transform their negative energy. There is so much wisdom in the video. It's a good one to watch. Big, big touch of agreement from Warick right now all the way down the right side of my face.

24 March 2021

Tonight, while Mum and Ray are away, I took the opportunity to sage the house again. Initially, I spent time sitting in the middle of the upstairs living area, listening to a *YouTube* track that you play when you cleanse a house. It's really lovely. I just sat, extending my senses to see what I could feel in the house. I felt Warick in my face, so I knew he was with me. I explored with my mind communicating to see if there were any spirits in the house and inviting them to gently touch me. A few times while sitting in different positions, I felt a very light touch on each hand. It was like a little insect. Each time I checked my hand, I could see nothing there. I think there is a spirit that resides in this house that touches me. I inquired whether it was the spirit of a child, teenager or adult but got no response. I invited the spirit who resides in the house to be my friend and let me get to know it. I then walked around the house with a smouldering sage stick, cleansing the house of negative energy no matter its source, and filling the house with love and light. When I finished and was walking around closing the house, something really interesting happened. The dog mattress that was in the laundry, on a dog bed, was now lying in the middle of the hallway. I was walking down the corridor in the dark so nearly tripped on it. I know the dogs didn't put it there because they are elderly—both eleven—and they don't drag the dog mattresses anywhere. Once, when Max was little, he pulled Rosie around the living room at Yarralumla while she was sitting on a blanket. But he hasn't done this for years. And I certainly didn't move it. I think the spirit that resides in this house put it there. I checked with Warick using the pendulum and got a medium intensity swinging movement that indicated the spirit that resides in this house put it there to let me know it's there. Not to hurt me. He indicated that the spirit is a male adult, the person who first owned the house. I also think the pressure I've been feeling around me since coming to the house is this spirit. I can feel the pressure again now lightly around my head. I've asked this spirit to let me know when he is around and to try and communicate with me. I said I hope he lets me get to know him over time and said he should not be frightened of me. It will be interesting to see how things go.

26 March 2021

Well, I've had just over a week and a half to myself here at our coastal home and I'm really going to miss the solitude. Its uncomplicated, apart from the dogs and roof leaks. Mum and Ray return today. I love being on my own because I can wake up, get a coffee, go back to bed, and write in my journal in absolute peace. I wouldn't want solitude all the time, just a good dose of it every now and again. Warick is with me for a while every night. This morning, I woke to feeling his vibration around my face and in my right hand, feet and root chakra. He gradually merged with my body. I experienced a surge of energy around my solar plexus which, according to Charlie, the spirit who channels through Mark Bedwood on *YouTube*, is where your energy comes from. This, I understand from Wendy and Phil Dykes from My Mediumship, is also where your soul is. The surge of energy moved upwards through my body, then Warick gradually moved my head. As he does this type of thing, I talk to myself in my mind, coaching my ego saying, 'It's okay' and, 'We want Warick to do this'. It's really interesting because last night when I couldn't sleep, I read some more of the Seth series. Seth said if you get your ego to want to be part of your quest, so what you want becomes a part of your egotistical concern, then you can advance more easily, and you don't have the ego to contend with as an adversary. He also talked about projection, astral travel and out-of-body experiences occurring in Jane's dreams. Her record of the dreams was very similar to the dreams I wrote about in the journal quite some time ago, when I described what it felt like moving through walls. Jane moved through mirrors and her dream jumped all around the place, as did mine. The timing and parallels between what I experience and the material in the Seth series is uncanny.

This week, for the first time in a few months I've been meditating each day and listening to chakra healing, house cleansing and throat chakra activation music during the day. I'm feeling a lot calmer in myself and I'm starting to be able to meditate a bit longer without my mind being too busy. I'm not where I was before things started to go wrong, but I'm slowly moving back in that direction.

30 March 2021

A couple of things worth mentioning. A few nights ago, when I woke early in the morning, Warick let me know he was there and in control by making me smile—really big. My whole face engaged in the smile. It was terrific! Previously, he has only managed a small smile, just of my mouth. Early this morning, once again Warick let me know he was already there and in position to move my face. I felt a surge of energy from my solar plexus chakra, then he moved my head, and I felt my facial features change. It's really interesting. I can't wait until he can do more, particularly being able to speak.

31 March 2021

Today, I experienced a high-pitched tone in my left ear and when I closed my eyes to focus on it, I saw nothing but red. I have no idea what this means.

4 April 2021

The beach still mesmerises me. Hi Warick, who just touched my right cheek to let me know he's there. And again now. It's like he agrees with what I just wrote. It's Easter Sunday and perfect weather here at Kianga. Twenty-seven degrees Celsius, almost no cloud, no wind, and beautiful seas. Although we have walked the dogs on the beach semi-regularly since moving here, and I walk past the beach at lunchtimes, today is the first day we've gone to the beach and just sat there looking at the waves and the ocean. It's incredible! The sound, the movement, the colour, and the smell. It pulls on all your senses. No fail, it puts me to sleep every time. When my head kept nodding, I slid down in my deck chair with my wide straw hat on and proceeded to go to sleep. When I woke, people I saw swimming before were mostly gone, replaced by half a dozen people standing in the water with long fishing rods and their dogs playing games in the sand. I love it. I can sit on the beach all day. Before nodding off, the shadow shapes I see kept letting me know they were there. It's funny because the brim of my straw hat is quite low so they kept moving just below the rim so I could see them. I'm sure they know when I can see them and where they need to move to catch my eye. I've also noticed they're very active on the beach. I think they want to share in the happy time. The same occurs when I go walking. During the night, Warick seems to have settled into a pattern of merging with, and moving, my head. I often also feel him in my eyes, forehead and throat. I still hear tones and feel Spirit energy touch me from time to time. I also get hot often when Warick arrives. What I encounter is not as diverse as it was before. I don't know whether that's because I've been going through a hard time the last few months, or whether what Warick is doing now is where the focus and effort needs to be for me to become comfortable with his sharing my physical body and at times taking control. I've also had a sore throat the last week or so. It hasn't turned into anything; it's just sore. I don't know whether it's because I've been feeling run down, or because I've been listening to quite a lot of throat chakra activation music and Warick's energy is sometimes in my throat.

6 April 2021

I started the night with a few specific questions in mind for Warick, so I used my old favourite brass pendulum. As I opened the black silk bag, I found the pendulum chain was knotted again. This has happened at least the last three or four times I've gone to use the pendulum. The chain has never knotted before, that I can remember. The first question I had for Warick was, 'Is this a sign that I no longer need the pendulum?' I got no response. I then probed with my mind to look into Elder's eyes to ask the same question, and I got a 'yes' with the pendulum. I then stroked the pendulum and asked if we could use it this time. I asked if my sore throat was because I'm run down, to which I got, 'No'. I got a 'yes' to the reason being because Warick is working with my throat chakra. I suspected this was the case. I asked if I should keep listening to the throat chakra activation meditation, to which I got, 'No', and the third eye activation, to which I also got, 'No'. I then asked if I should listen to a heart chakra activation meditation, to which I got, 'Yes'. Just recently, when walking at the beach, I collected a brown feather, which may have come from an eagle. I already have a white feather, and a black and white feather. Elder confirmed using the pendulum that the white feather means an angel is with me, the brown feather means Elder is with me, and the black and white feather means I need balance with Spirit in my life.

Once again, as occurred on 31 March, I experienced a high-pitched tone in my left ear and when I closed my eyes, I saw red. Something else I noticed when I woke the other night and was experiencing Warick's spirit, I caught the sound of him taking in a breath. It was very distinct, quite loud and definitely coming from my mouth at the time I took a breath. I breathe very quietly. In fact, I'm almost silent. I know this was the sound of Warick taking a breath through my body. It's very special.

I have noticed this before and thought the same thing at the time, but this time I'm certain of it. It's wonderful and amazing. It makes it all so very real, to be sharing this physical body with another spirit. It's a big decision to share your physical body with another spirit. It requires love more than anything.

10 April 2021

Warick is continuing his merging activities with me during the night. It feels like my face is taking on his facial features. It feels like your skin is being stretched in different directions. There is also his taking control of where he moves my head and uses my mouth to smile. The fact that it is such a gradual process, and frequent—occurring most nights—is enabling me to get used to it and be comfortable with it. I'm intrigued with what he is doing and where this is all headed. I also often feel the lower part of my calf muscles, near my ankles, clench and tighten. This is hard to describe, and I don't know what is happening. Possibly it's Warick's energy extending through my body, I don't know. Maybe in time this will become clear, but for now my immediate reaction is concern that the muscles will cramp painfully, which is not good because it distracts me from being relaxed with what Warick is doing. Last night, I also felt a light energy touch the back left of my head, like the touch of a hand in energy form.

Yesterday at lunchtime was interesting. During my walk at the lake in Canberra, I sat for about ten minutes at a favourite viewpoint. My eyes were closed for most of the time and once again, I saw red, but then I saw a beautiful bright light blue and then deeper purple. It was really interesting. I don't know what it means.

11 April 2021

It's Sunday night and I'm finally finding time to start typing up the next journal. I haven't been feeling well for several weeks now. Sore throat, tiredness and headaches. Anyway, I haven't had the energy to start typing up the journal. I want so much to get back into the routine of typing up journals and sharing sections as I type them up with John to read. Several times, what I type up seems to be linked with John experiencing things. It's fascinating. Anyway, I subscribe to the Huff Paranormal *YouTube* channel. As I was sitting down tonight to type up more of the journal, I received a notification that Steve Huff had posted another video. He was riding around his property with an EVP recorder. At one stop, he asked, 'Is love the key to connection with Spirit?' and the response he got on the EVP recorder was, 'That is when they go into you.' This makes a lot of sense to me. From the beginning, it was, and continues to be, the love I feel for Warick that coincides with his energy coming into my body. It's when I asked him to say 'love' that he gave me this incredible sensation welling up from my heart to my throat chakra. What the spirits told Huff is exactly it. It's your love for them that enables their energy to come in and interact with you. It's wonderful and it's great to have this verified through Steve Huff's video. Steve, like me, was keen to know if our connection with Spirit will continue to grow, to which Spirit responded to Steve saying, 'Yes.' I find this interesting because I suspect many, if not all, people who truly experience Spirit, want the connection to continue to grow and evolve. It's like an addiction and you can't get enough. You want more and you want more diversity. I don't know why, but this feeling is very real and at times frustrating.

13 April 2021

Just a very brief note to say that last night as I felt Warick's energy in my face, he managed to open my mouth a few times. He just touched my cheek now to confirm this. Very exciting! Only in the one direction—'open'—but this is certainly progress. It was fine and I didn't feel awkward. He does these things seamlessly. My mind didn't fight him doing this at all, which is great. Another touch on the right cheek, also agreeing with this observation.

14 April 2021

It gets confusing as I type up previous journal entries into a book manuscript. In a sense, I'm reliving my experiences and thoughts, and Warick starts to touch my right cheek confirming things I thought previously. It makes me laugh. I love that he is with me. Right now, I'm shaking my head and having a chuckle because we are essentially adding a layer of thought and complexity to what I've already recorded in a journal. For example, on 17 September 2020, when I wrote about the reactions I got from a table of friends when I asked them what they thought the purpose of life was, Warick touched my right cheek confirming my thoughts that the purpose of life is to learn lessons, good and bad, to evolve your soul. It's wonderful that he confirms this for many reasons, but largely because this is also the message I want humanity to know. It's an interesting process, typing up journal entries from past experiences while also recording Warick's response to what I'm typing up now. While typing up the 20 September 2020 entry, I came across my experience of itchy skin associated with spiritual awakening and … of course, about ten minutes ago, I was scratching the left area of my forehead. Now, I'm typing up an entry about how you can sense the feelings of others around you, and Warick is touching my right cheek saying, 'This is what has been happening to you lately.' I know! I know! I know! I think I have a way to go before I'm on top of how to love those around me but not let their negative feelings impact on my health and happiness. This is a trait Mum also needs to learn. Maybe we could work at it together.

17 April 2021

Tonight was significant. Tomorrow, finally John, Jules, Jane, and I will sit in a circle. A circle that is spread across the world, but there you have it. I don't know the significance of this. I have not been well for weeks. Feeling run down and an achy throat. Not like tonsilitis. Just achy. Particularly in the afternoons when my voice starts to go. This could be completely unrelated to what has occurred tonight. I took a bath earlier this evening. We have a beautiful bath at Yarralumla. It's more like something from a spa resort. Beautiful deep, large bath set into a tiled area. The tiles are like natural stone running up to the ceiling. There is a sunken cove in the wall next to the bath with down lights, a beautiful authentic Buddha face at peace, candles, and incense. Incredibly peaceful. While I was lying in the bath with milk powder, candles and incense burning, and listening to music on *YouTube*, I started to think about Warick. I immediately saw Warick lying still on a flat platform. His eyes were closed, and he was completely still. I thought he was asleep, so I started to gently kiss his cheeks and whispered, 'Warick' in his ear to try and wake him. It took me a while to realise he was dead. I didn't feel pain associated with his state. I was at peace with him. He was about forty years old. Mature, but not old. Handsome and strong. I knew he had died of a sickness. I don't know how I knew this or what type of disease it was. I was completely at peace with him. No one that I was aware of was there. I vowed eternal love to him. I realised this is what infinity had meant. Our souls, our spirits, forever intertwined. I can't remember all my thoughts, but Warick was with me because as I was thinking things, he gently touched my right cheek confirming my thoughts. I have no idea if this is meant to coincide with our circle tomorrow. What I saw is hugely significant. Not only because of what it is, but also because when Warick had shown me Elder's, and then my, death, I wondered why he hadn't shown me his. I have often wondered why and thought maybe there is a block, because it would be too painful for me to bear. I felt no pain though, only peace. Not joyful, but peace. I also felt determination and commitment of my eternal love and connection with him.

The last week has been interesting. Rosie, one of my dogs, who is highly perceptive of humans, has been hanging around me like she has never done before. So much so, Ray recognised it as well. At first, I thought she wasn't well and was trying to tell me, but that's not it. I tried asking Warick with the pendulum. His response was she didn't need a vet, that she detected I was trying to communicate with her. Warick said I would understand her at some stage. I have no idea why she was like this for a few days. She just stuck with me, wanting to be close and staring at me, not shifting her gaze. She is usually incredibly independent. I wonder if she sensed something leading to this significant event with Warick. And I wonder if my sickness is also somehow related. I don't know.

18 April 2021

I'm sick. When I woke, my throat was much worse. No fever or symptoms of a cold or flu, but it was clear my throat was worse. You could hear it in my voice. Ray said, 'You need to go to the doctor' and looked up our medical centre opening hours. After a shower, I headed straight there, and because it involved the throat and wariness about COVID, I had to wait in the car for my appointment. I was lucky because our doctor was working, and I managed to get an appointment with him. I had to wait nearly two hours but that was just fine. I trust him. He is a really good doctor. He detected Ray's myeloma cancer while he was looking into something else. He said I had no temperature, but my throat was red and possibly infected, so he prescribed antibiotics. Because I live with two COVID high-risk people, he said I should get a COVID test to be safe, so I went to a walk-in clinic that does COVID testing. Now the big wait for the test result. I should be okay as I already live in a very cautious way with work-from-home arrangements, but we shall see. I feel like I've let many people down today. I had to cancel Warick's circle session with John, Jules and Jane. All were very understanding, which I was really grateful for, and they are happy to reschedule to when I'm better. This is the second time I've cancelled so I'm not feeling very happy with myself.

Last night, after the experience in the bath where I saw Warick dead and knew he had died from a sickness, I emailed and let John, Jules and Jane know as I said I'd share anything that I experienced ahead of the circle meeting in case it was related. Jane responded with a couple of messages, including one where she said by showing me his death it was clear Warick knew today's circle meeting would not occur, and he wants me to rest up and get better. It was possibly Warick giving me a sign. Jane suggested I ask Warick for some healing love, so I did. Mentally, I asked Warick and Elder if they could help heal me. This afternoon, while resting in bed, I had a wonderful experience, where I think Warick and possibly other spirits were helping me. For the past two and a half hours, I've been listening to a meditation track called 'The Deepest Healing Sleep/3.2 Hz Delta Brain Waves'. I wanted to relax and possibly sleep. I don't think I slept, but I reached an incredibly relaxed state. I felt Warick's energy come completely over the top of me and merge with my body all over. I also felt a strong connection through my root chakra that stayed there pretty much the whole time. I felt Warick touch my right cheek, letting me know he was there and that it was alright. He moved my head gently and opened my mouth slightly. I just went with it, completely trusting him and just letting go. After a while, I felt a pull-down sensation from the base of my throat, under my voice box that moved to my chest, specifically between my ribs at the base of my rib cage between my breasts. It hurt and was painful. I was okay, but it wasn't pleasant. I then felt it moving towards the back of me, specifically to a spot at the base of my left shoulder blade. I've experienced pain in this spot before and wondered what it was. The pain lasted numerous minutes. I continued to feel Warick's energy merged with mine throughout my body. After a while, I felt this pulling sensation, like his energy was being extracted slowly upwards out of my body. This sensation continued for a minute or so. I started to feel uncomfortably hot, so I threw the covers off and sat up. I leaned over and pressed stop on the meditation track. I was amazed to see that it had stopped almost exactly halfway through the meditation track, 2:25:25 of 4:59:59 to be exact, and that the numbers were repetitive. I don't know what the significance of this is but it's interesting. Possibly Warick confirming he was with me and that what I had just experienced was Spirit helping to heal me. As I type this up, over a year later, Warick has just touched my right cheek, I suspect confirming that yes, Warick was with me and helped me to heal, and that this is possibly what the repetitive numbers meant. I'll have to share this with John, Jules and Jane. I remember a repeated numbers experience occurred last time I linked up with Jules, plus John and I have shared 11:11 and infinity experiences as well. Encounters with Spirit never cease to amaze me.

29 April 2021

If I express love within myself towards my soul family—Warick, Elder and Wolf—it takes me straight to them. I connect with them. I feel Warick within my face and I quickly see them in my mind. I just start talking to them in my mind in a loving way and this is what happens.

Tonight is important. Together we discovered the key for me to let go with confidence and let Warick take control easily and fluidly. Their idea, I'm sure, and that's just fine. We are a team. I started by thinking loving thoughts with no music. I just started talking to them about what they mean to me, which connected me to them. I felt Warick and saw Elder and Wolf. I used what I had learned in the 'Sitting in the Power' workshop this week to visualise the light at a distance in the dark. It cast rays of light in all directions, including in my direction where some rays fell on me. I remembered the time when Warick, Elder and I held hands while standing side by side looking at the sun setting over the ocean during a meditation session last year. One of the most beautiful experiences I've had in my life. We were completely at peace with each other. A knowing shared between us. Tonight, as I stood in the dark looking at the source of light casting rays in all directions, once again Warick and Elder were at my sides holding my hands. The experience was the same as it was over a year ago when we looked at the sun setting over the ocean. This was the key to what was about to transpire. Suddenly, I was behind us looking at the three of us standing together and looking away from me at the light. It was like my consciousness split where part of it was observing myself from behind my physical body, and at the same time I could feel Warick within my face in front of me moving fluidly in all directions. This went on for numerous minutes, where I was completely relaxed and happy for Warick to do what he was doing because I could still see myself standing in front of me. I felt completely safe. This line of strength and love standing in front of me was like a wall of protection. Nothing was going to harm me in that moment. I don't know why it felt like this, but it did. Wonderful! The key to overcoming my fear of Warick taking control of my body! They are so imaginative and clever and do things smoothly with grace. I love them so very much. Amazing!

3 May 2021

These are interesting times indeed. To recap, since 2013, I've experienced Spirit in some way almost every day. Initially, during the night, as energy vibration in localised spots near me so I was aware of its presence, but it did not touch me. At the time, I was conscious, and I could feel localised vibration. I literally spent months looking for a logical explanation for it. Then, on 14 January 2014, for the first time, Spirit let me touch its energy, just a few hours before Dad unexpectedly died. At this moment, I knew beyond doubt that intelligent energy exists. It wanted me to know it exists and knew that I would not have a logical explanation for it. An unseen intelligent energy, which is way beyond what science educates children about in school. I knew the significance of this. It blew me away!

Two years later, for some reason in early June 2018, I had a full-on encounter with spirit energy in a sexually stimulating way. It was almost non-stop stimulation of my sexual organs over a period of about two weeks. It completely exhausted me. I could feel localised energy move from the entry of my vagina, through to the cervix and into the cervical canal. It's very possible that it moved into the endometrium, uterus and the fallopian tubes, because I could feel the energy travel well past the cervix. I've never experienced a sensation in these parts of my body before though, so I can't be sure exactly where it reached. I have no doubt that it was intentionally stimulating me through the path of my sexual organs and sometimes pausing in locations and doubling back. The encounters weren't meant to be like a human making love with another human. It was different, but the energy's intention was clearly to stimulate my sexual organs. The intensity and sensations I experienced were absolutely incredible. I got so sleep deprived during this time that eventually I had to say to the spirit, 'If you don't settle down, you're going to have to leave.' It was getting too much.

After this period, I experienced the most amazing exponential spiritual growth with an incredible diversity of spiritual encounters, some of which involved linkage to other people, including my aunt's passing, as well as John, Jules and Jane. Late in 2020, when for personal reasons of going through a significant change in living circumstances, which impacted heavily on Mum, Ray and myself, Spirit engagement was still there every day and every night, but it was far less diverse. Which brings me to now. I've sent the first journal, typed up as a book, to numerous publishers and literary agents, none of which have yet been interested in helping me to publish it. Knowing what I know now about the existence of Spirit—as someone who did not go looking for it, who is part of the human race that either don't believe, or have doubts about the spirit world, who believes only what science has proven as fact and teaches us at school; I'm quite dumbfounded that something as important as this at the end of the day, will come down to a few publishers who read the manuscript, find it interesting and want to publish it. It just seems so ridiculous! I'm also starting to realise how un-unique my experiences are, so why write about it? I've always known other people claim to experience things, and I'm sure in many cases they do, and way beyond what I have. I suppose a key part of my wanting to publish this material is because I want to contribute what I can to what will lead others to knowing for sure that intelligent energy exists. I'm sitting here shaking my head and starting to laugh. Just as much as I love Warick, Elder and Wolf, I also want humanity to wake up to itself. You never know, just like some famous artist, this material may not become well known until I'm well and truly gone. In which case, at least I feel like I've done the right thing, having been so diligent in recording these events to the best of my ability for my son, who I wanted to share them with originally, and for John, who encouraged me to write them up as books, and is part of the journey. Today, while sitting on the sand for a while during my lunchtime walk, I felt Warick come into my face as I stared at the sea and then closed my eyes to listen to the waves. I thought to myself, I'm in a place which, for many years, brought me peace and happiness, and now Warick is here. His energy also appears in my face when I look at a beautiful sunrise, and like tonight, also while sitting on the front deck listening to the thunder and rain and watching the lightning across the ocean. Warick usually makes his presence known by moving within my face when I experience these wonderful moments in nature that he knows I love so much. He is still with me almost every night.

When I wake through the night, I feel him move within my face and sometimes my body. Sometimes my temperature also goes up with these occurrences. I still see shadow shapes around me every day, which are particularly noticeable when I go walking and while I'm in the office working and listening to beautiful piano music. I also still experience pressure on one side of my head or the other, often accompanied by a tone that lasts several seconds, and sometimes it occurs again shortly after. In my next entry, I'll include what I've experienced during the 'Sitting in the Power' sessions number two and three.

I've recently started reading a book called, *DESTINY OF SOULS: New Case Studies of Life Between Lives* authored by Michael Newton PhD and published by Llewellyn Publications Woodbury, Minnesota, which is really interesting and based on hundreds of case studies of his clients' subconscious recollections of their life between lives. I've just started reading it, but straight away it was helpful as he talked about his findings of associating colours of spirit energy with how mature a spirit is. A highly advanced spirit is purple, which I've seen a lot of when in the session with Jane and at other times, which I associate with Warick. He claims immature spirits are white and then progress through colours of orange, red, green, and blues as they become more advanced. I don't know which spirit I saw that presented itself as a white panel of light, with shimmering sides, in the shower at Amooran one time on my own, but I assumed it was Warick. The other colours I've seen at times in my mind's eye with my eyes closed. I've seen a lot of purple, and beautiful peacock blue and red. I may have seen other colours and mentioned them in the journal, but these are the ones I recollect. I can't remember it exactly, but he also described spirits as light intelligent energy. I find it reassuring that another person describes Spirit in this way. I know many others describe Spirit as energy, and that everything is energy, but Spirit is a unique form of energy, which is intelligent, and their abilities are incredible. It's clear from reading Michael's book that his recordings are legitimate. He also talks about you having a soul group, which makes me think Warick, Elder and Wolf are possibly my soul group. And as usual, wonderful timing—I've just experienced a touch on my right check from Warick confirming this.

4 May 2021

Before I continue reading the book, *DESTINY OF SOULS* by Michael Newton, I must share with you an experience I had while reading the book. It's the middle of the night—3.03 am to be precise. I'm sure Warick led me to purchase this book. It's incredible! The chapter I'm reading now includes a section called, 'Ways spirits connect with the living', which validates the diversity of ways I've experienced Warick. It refers to the incredible range of things Spirit can do with energy, which has blown me away from the beginning. I felt Warick in my face as I was reading this section of the book and he responded to my questions as they came to mind. For example, after reading an account where a client, having a life between lives experience, said when he died and visited his wife, he would meld his energy with a fire his wife was staring into. I asked Warick if this is what he does when I gaze at the falling water in the shower, to which he replied, 'Yes' by touching my right cheek. This client went on to describe how he connected with his wife's mind by directing part of his energy into a ring he used to wear, which encouraged her to pick it up. He then formed what he called 'an energy bridge' between the residual energy he left in the ring that lay in her hand, and himself as energy on the other side of her. She then sensed and acknowledged that she knew he was there. At that very moment, while reading this part, Warick sent a very strong tingling sensation through my body and left me with a very distinct feeling of peace. I told him how much I love him and apologised for my busy mind that has been jumping around a lot lately with work, home and other matters. Now I've just read an account where a recently departed soul turned on a music box that hadn't been touched in years; to play a song his wife would associate with him. She was sitting in the room at the time, saying to her friends how she 'hadn't experienced any sign from her husband since he had died'. Of course, this reminded me of the music box that turned itself on one day when I was working shortly after Dad died. It hasn't been turned on in years. I'm sure Warick guided me to this book to confirm what I suspected from my own experiences and to learn from other's experiences. He is wonderful!

Tonight, was the last of three 'Sitting in the Power' workshops I've done with Phil Dykes and Kerry McLeod from My Mediumship. I feel Warick in my face now, so he is obviously interested to see what I write about it. He was with me for much of it, so I think he knows already. It was terrific. I have a much better understanding now about the purpose of the stages of 'Sitting in the Power'. Going from initially sitting in your own power of self and learning how to hold that and build your sensitivities, to then going a little further, probing out with your energy and senses, and allowing Spirit to come in and interact with you. I do see the value now of regularly doing this. Tonight, during the 'Sitting in the Power' workshop, I felt Warick's energy across my cheeks, eyes and forehead. At times, I felt at complete peace with him, which was lovely. I think we are learning to be at complete peace with each other for longer durations of time. Now, all I need to do is make it a priority most days to find an hour to sit with Spirit. Phil Dykes and Kerry McLeod from My Mediumship said your guides will evolve what happens when you do this practice.

On a totally different subject, today I noticed a magpie sitting on a sign at the beach that watched me as I went by. It was really interesting because it was still there about thirty minutes later when I walked back the other way. I asked, 'Are you still there?' I've never known a bird in the wild to sit for so long in a spot like that or possibly return to the exact same spot a while later. There were no trees around; it was completely in the open on the beach front. Plus, it's not the season for them to be protecting their young. It was very strange. So strange, I thought it was worth noting.

5 May 2021

Warick is certainly working on my throat. Last night when I woke, I reached out to Warick with my mind. I focused on that stage of 'Sitting in the Power' where you sense self first. I know Warick was already there, but I suspect he was being polite, allowing me to put into practice what I'd learned. Knowing Warick was there, I moved to reaching out to him in my mind and allowing him to interact with me. As I got into a very relaxed state, I kept being interrupted by a sound coming from my voice box. Warick is touching my right cheek now so is confirming this. It's like Phil Dykes and Kerry McLeod from My Mediumship said—when you're in a very relaxed state and engaging with Spirit, your senses are much more sensitive, so the sound coming from my voice box disturbed me a little each time it happened. It took me a while to realise what Warick was doing. He made this sound with my voice box time and time again—about ten times. It's hard to describe, but it's like the short sound you make when you clear your throat. I also noticed when he made this noise that it was just when I was drifting off to sleep. My throat feels a little raspy this morning. I do wonder if this is why I've been having trouble with my throat lately. Ever since the infection in my throat has cleared up with antibiotics, it's still a little sore around the voice box every day. My doctor has given me a referral to see a specialist in August.

7 May 2021

Another wonderful example of Warick's carefully orchestrated sequence of events for my learning benefit, happened tonight as I was typing up more entries from my last journal in a book that will be called *AWAKENING II - 1NF1N1T1*. It was an account of Warick and I doing the most amazing risky moves while ice skating as I daydreamed walking near the lake at lunchtime. At the time, I wondered if Warick was doing this to build my trust in him because as a little girl I was petrified of being lifted above the men's heads when doing various lifts and jumps in ballet. While typing this up, I remembered Phil Dykes said at the last 'Sitting in the Power' session, that Spirit will work out what you're most frightened of and use it to gain your trust in them. It confirmed what I thought Warick was doing with me in the ice-skating daydreams. This is incredible. It's like Warick knew I would be typing up the experience I had with him previously in the same week that I would be told by Phil Dykes that spirits use what they know you are afraid of to gain your trust. Essentially, two sources telling me the same thing. But also, Warick possibly using the timing of what Phil Dykes would say to confirm what he did to gain my trust. I was so excited about this discovery that I sent Phil Dykes and Kerry McLeod from My Mediumship the journal entry to say thank you for what I had learned from them in the 'Sitting in the Power' workshop, and to share what had just happened.

Also, something interesting happened at lunchtime when I was meditating to 'Light Activation' by Spiritual Zen on *YouTube*, which is one of my favourites. I was sitting in a chair in the office with my eyes closed, and I saw glimpses of the most beautiful, glowing, blue colour. When I tilted my head down with my eyes still closed, the glowing blue appeared to be emanating from my body. I could see it glowing from the edges of my body through my mind's eye. I'm wondering if blue is the colour of my spirit or aura. It was a beautiful deep peacock blue and was glowing brightly. When I moved my hand that was resting in my lap, even with my eyes closed, I could make out the glowing blue around my hand. It was like I was looking at myself with night goggles on, but what I saw was this beautiful, bright, glowing blue colour all down my body. Incredible!

15 May 2021

Last night, something new happened. And you know how much I love and crave new forms of engagement to occur with Spirit. I have this habit when I wake during the night where I reach out with my mind to see if Warick is there. I ask, 'Are you with me now, Warick?' He must get tired of me saying this because it occurs multiple times every night and has been going on for years. Anyway, last night when I woke and started to reach out in my mind to Warick, I saw this very fast flash of a neon sign in my mind's eye. It was a black sign with white neon writing saying, 'WELCOME BACK' in capital letters. It was so fast I almost missed it. Warick is touching my right cheek now confirming this is what happened. As soon as I saw the sign, I reached out in my mind and asked, 'Did you just show me an image of a neon sign saying, 'WELCOME BACK'? Immediately, Warick touched my right cheek confirming he did. I thought it was quite funny. He was obviously ready and waiting for me to wake up and reach out to see if he was there, and to show me the sign. He had to time it perfectly. He only had a split second to show me the sign. I asked Warick if he could leave the sign there longer next time as I almost missed it.

17 May 2021

Tonight, while practicing 'Sitting in the Power' meditation with no music, in my mind's eye Elder and Warick joined me on either side while I was standing looking at the light off in the distance. We held hands. All just staring at the light. We were in darkness and could see streams of light energy come out from the source of light. We moved closer. I thought to myself, *The light source seems to be alive.* Tuning into my thoughts, Elder confirmed this and said, 'It is alive. It's our home. When we are there, the light of our spirit contributes to the overall light, which is what we are looking at now. The light is our pooled light energy of all the spirits residing within it. Don't feel anxious about the light. It's full of love and happiness. When you're not in the light, you're living a physical existence.'

The other night, a strange thing happened. I woke up to what I thought was the sound of my own voice, but it wasn't my voice. It sounded like a scrambled male's voice, and it came from me. It's possible I dreamt it, but it seemed real. It was very brief, and I was immediately concerned that I'd wake Ray. It will be interesting to see if this happens again.

20 May 2021

Tonight, I'm sure it will be impossible to sleep. I think I'm close to a job offer and I'm feeling uneasy. I don't know why, possibly because it's another big change and everything hasn't been right for many months on many fronts. I want so much for things to be settled and happy. Not just for me but also for Mum, Ray and our crazy dogs, who I know have also been going through significant change since moving to Kianga. I want to feel safe in what we now have, which is so special. Comfortable, so I can relax and be happy. Despite all my probing, Warick has not given anything away as to whether a job with a small consultancy company is the right move. His responses have been unclear. The decision is mine. It seems right and the feeling seems mutual with the partners of the company. It seems too good to be true, which also makes me feel a bit wary. I'll have to wait and see. Referee checks are next, but they have said they are keen to take me on, and we have agreed on a salary, so fingers crossed it will all come together. Ray is in Canberra tonight, so I had the opportunity to sit in the quiet in the centre of the house in the dark, and near the warmth of the heater. I wanted to see what I could feel. Warick made his presence known by moving his energy around in my face. I sensed the resident Spirit at one stage. It was a peaceful, slight vacuum feeling in front of me, to which I greeted and said, 'You're always welcome to engage with me.' Now I'm feeling a push on my left shoulder blade, which I think is Spirit letting me know it's there and trying to get my attention. Interestingly, tonight Warick also gradually opened my mouth when I was sitting on the chair in the middle of the house in the dark. I felt warmth towards the top inside of my mouth several times, and a slight vibration inside my mouth and around some of my teeth. It was very distinct and obvious. It always interests me what Spirit does, and it makes me wonder why. It's been a happy day. Something I'm very thankful for.

21 May 2021

This morning before dawn, I woke to feeling Warick's gentle vibration around the back of my head and slightly to the left. I asked Warick if he wanted to merge with me, then I felt his energy move through me. The sensation was mostly in my head, but I also felt a slight pressure in the centre of my forehead and at my root chakra, as though it was extending down from my root chakra. My mind was quite busy, which was not good, but then I saw an image of Elder with his eyes closed and that helped me to focus. Each time I realised my thoughts had wandered off, I brought my focus back to the memory of seeing Elder. At one stage, I felt Warick touch my right cheek. I think he was encouraging me, telling me I'm doing fine. Warick moved my head gently a few times. I could also sense he wanted me to open my mouth, so I parted my lips slightly where I could hear myself breathing. About four or five times when my mind was relaxed but distracted, Warick made the noise he's made before using my voice box. There's no specific word. It's more like he's practising getting sound to come out of it. It's very brief and brings my attention back to what he's doing. He then showed me in my mind's eye an image of red poppies quickly coming up among blue flowers. The field of view of the image was, I'd say, the same as when he showed me the neon sign with the words, 'WELCOME BACK' on it. It's a rectangular shape with black surrounding it. Today, the flowers took up my entire field of view. I can understand now why some people say what you see in your mind's eye is like a movie screen. The first time the screen was completely black with the words, 'WELCOME BACK' in bright, white, neon letters and everything beyond the screen was also black. Today, once again, everything beyond the rectangular screen was black and the flowers completely covered the screen. It was also interesting that the red poppies quickly moved up through the blue flowers, so I was seeing a moving image on the screen. I don't know what this means. Maybe Warick was rewarding my efforts with him as he tries to make sound from my voice box. I love flowers. I'm so glad Warick and Elder are in my life.

22 May 2021

Okay, I stand corrected. I'm just typing up the next journal, and last year in September I did make an entry about seeing in my mind's eye a drawing of an elephant, which moved. Seeing the poppies rise through the blue flowers is not the first time I've seen an image in my mind's eye, move. Reflecting on it, I suppose red poppies rising through blue flowers could signify you're coming through the blue times. Things will be bright and happy again. Or, it could have been a warning about not falling into the trap of the 'tall poppy syndrome'. Now Warick is touching my right cheek, so I suspect this is the message they are sending me. I've had a lot of interest in me lately—from recruitment agencies and possible future employers. I need to make sure it doesn't go to my head. I need to focus on what's important. Remain humble and thankful. I think I've been okay. I'm trying to make sure I choose the right path. I love Mum and Ray for coming on this journey with me. It's been hard for them. To have a happy life living between the coast and Canberra, it's important that I get the balance right between where I work and where I live. I've had a very open discussion about this with the partners of the consultancy company, and they seem understanding, accepting and comfortable with this. I also need to be flexible by being available when one of the partners wants to discuss something on a weekend. They need to know I'm reliable and there to help take the business forward. It's a different mindset compared to being a contractor for a global defence industry company.

25 May 2021

Sometimes extreme frustration, combined with problem solving, pushes through the answer. I found it so frustrating not knowing why Spirit came to me in a major way in June 2018. Although time has passed, Warick is still clearly here, and he is touching my right cheek now to confirm this. The diversity and intensity of the encounters have settled down compared with the rapid pace initially. Tonight, I pulled out the pendulum to explore some things with Warick. I got it wrong in the preface that I wrote for the first book. What is happening between Warick and I; it's not for the good of humanity—it's for the good of the source of Spirit. This clarification is so important that I had to write it down immediately. We aren't here for humanity's sake; we are here for the sake of the source of Spirit. Now I understand why so many mediums are passionate about being 'in service' of Spirit. Not that I feel totally comfortable with this, as it's like they are opening themselves up as vessels with no intelligence or part to play. I suspect there is another learning in this for me.

4 June 2021

It's been difficult deciding whether to record my recollections of a couple of past life regression sessions with Joe Tracy on *YouTube*. In the end, I decided I would, because they are interesting and I don't know where they are going—if anywhere. By now, you are on this journey with me, so here we go, whether it is real or not. As you know, I'll be the first one to call it out if I think it's not real or if I have doubt. I do know that Warick and Elder leverage my meditative states, guided or unguided, to piggyback off my imagination to then show me what they want to. Sometimes I don't imagine anything, and scenes just appear that they want to show me. Over the past week, when awake in the middle of the night, I've done a couple of Joe Tracy's past life regression *YouTube* videos. I particularly like his voice and the background noises he uses. It's easy to relax, and his voice is nice to listen to. During the meditation, Joe starts by relaxing you, then he gets you to visualise a passageway of doors where each door represents the entrance to one of your past lives. He gets you to identify a door that for some reason appeals to you. He doesn't describe the doors. You imagine them. On the first night, the door that appealed to me was like the trunk of a very large ancient tree. I stepped inside and found myself in a familiar environment with Warick and Elder. It was the ancient forest. I should have recorded this experience the next day when the memories were fresh in my mind, but from what I can remember in this past life, it was clear Elder was trying to teach me something involving a smoking pipe. It seemed ritualistic. Something about connecting with Spirit. When Joe progressed me to another event in that lifetime, I was standing on the forest floor staring up through the canopy of a tree to the sky. It was incredible and I was mesmerized by it. For some reason standing on the floor of an ancient forest and looking up through the beautiful green-coloured leaves that were highlighted by the sunlight, to the sky beyond, had me at a standstill. It was incredibly significant at the time. I know Warick was somewhere close by watching me but not interfering. This is so typical of him. He often watches me and says nothing. It's Elder who communicates with me. Passes on wisdom, teaches, and guides me. Right at the end of the session, it occurred to me that maybe I was being trained by Elder to be a sharman for our village. It seemed to fit with the smoke ceremony.

The second past life regression session I've done with Joe Tracy this week is in some ways even more interesting. This time, in the passageway, my imagination conjured up a glass-panelled door where I could see what I thought were clouds on the other side. When I walked through the door, I discovered the clouds were actually mist. I was high in the mountains. When I looked to the right at the top of an adjoining mountain top, there was an ancient temple that was open on one side facing spectacular views of the mountains and valleys below. I walked up to the temple and soon found myself on the platform looking at the view. Elder was standing on one side staring at me. He had an Indian blanket around his shoulders. Warick was on the other side of the platform, also staring at me. He was standing there, chest bare, looking strong and just staring at me. Joe, in the meditation, got you to briefly look at yourself to see what you looked like—your age, what you were wearing and what you were doing. I was about thirty. I had long, dark hair, plaited on one side with leather or cloth woven through it. I was wearing moccasin shoes and a native American Indian dress. I was unusually beautiful. I seemed completely at ease, happily going about my business. In a graceful way, I was looking through, and writing in, a large ancient journal as though it was my job to do so. The journal was open on a pedestal in the centre of the temple. It's like the temple was the sacred place where this work was done. Built for this purpose. Warick and Elder were standing by, watching me like it was their job to do so. When I looked at Warick, it occurred to me that he isn't my spirit guide; he is my protector. I remember Jules said to me in the first session with her, that Warick wanted me to know he will protect me. Rarely has he tried to guide me. This seems to be Elder's role—to guide and teach me. He is my mentor and passes on wisdom, whereas Warick protects and loves me. With both, an unbreakable bond and love that lasts through lifetimes. Just before coming out of the meditation, I was trying to work out the purpose of the journal. I wondered, if I was a sharman, was it a log of information that I was keeping for our village?

Maybe the past life regression experiences I've had this week have provided glimpses of who I am. It's clear Warick is staying tight lipped about it, because when I was using the pendulum tonight to check a few things with him, he was happy to confirm he is my protector, and that Elder is a teacher, but he would not let on about the nature of the journal on the pedestal. I asked if it was an Akashic record or journal that I was responsible for as a sharman. The pendulum went still and would not respond. I tried a few times and when it came to this question, the pendulum went completely still. I find it interesting that rarely do I have scenes of a village, or other people coming into my meditation and past life regression experiences. I'm mostly alone with Warick, Elder, Wolf, Falcon, and sometimes Horse. We are usually in nature, in the wilderness somewhere.

I've recently bought a beautiful and unusual statue of Venus. I didn't know it was Venus until I got the statue home and looked on the box to see what it was called. I'm wondering if there's a message or connection here. I need to do some research on Venus.

5 June 2021

Last night, when I couldn't sleep, I did another of Joe Tracy's past life regression meditation tracks designed to discover your life's purpose. It was interesting. When I went through a door in a wall at the bottom of ten stone steps in the middle of an ancient forest, I came out in another ancient forest that was even older than the one I had just come from. Joe guides you to the bottom of the steps and the door but then your imagination takes over when you walk through it. The forest was thick with ancient trees where their roots were exposed and almost joining together. I saw Elder, Warick and Wolf, and Falcon was on Warick's shoulder. Elder was busily tending to a small fire on the ground in between some large, exposed roots. Warick stood by and watched. Shortly after, in the distance, but not too far away, I saw another two old native American Indians who had blankets around their shoulders. They were just standing there and looking at us. While I was looking at them, Joe said something about 'your soul family can be there'. I haven't seen them before. Joe then got you to walk through another door. As I did, I found myself standing in a field of grass on the top of a hill. It was like a large, clear mound on the top of a hill with no trees or boulders. The grass was not too long. It was a beautiful, lush, green colour. While standing there, I encountered a column of white light, which I immediately associated with the Lord God. He started to pace backwards and forwards in front of me, with his hands clasped together. I found this interesting because I knew it was the Lord, but I didn't go looking for him, let alone do I even know if I believe in him. When I asked him what my life's purpose is, I immediately thought, 'To love'. He said he is in me, that I am a part of him. He said my path is set, and that I'm on the right path. This all seemed very vague to me. I wondered if I'm supposed to do something or achieve something. My thoughts turned to my book and, reading my mind, he said, 'Yes, you should continue with that, as you enjoy writing.' It seemed like this was not a primary thought for him. As though it didn't matter too much. I felt a little disappointed as what he conveyed was general and obvious. I don't know if what I'm experiencing in these meditations is true or has significance in a spiritual engagement sense. But it is interesting, and I will continue to record these experiences to see if they become important in some way. Joe Tracy is certainly not getting me to visualise the encounters I'm having, and they seem to come into my mind with ease and fluidity. They aren't experiences that I've thought about in any way. We shall see.

9 June 2021

A quick note, as this may already be captured in the journal. A few weeks ago, when I woke to a terrible cramp in my left calf muscle in the middle of the night, the pain was that bad I was not able to concentrate and use my mind to start relaxing the muscle. I reached out with my right hand and gently touched the muscle just below the back of my knee. I felt energy flow through my hand into the muscle, and I immediately started to feel the cramp let go. Where the cramp let go, it corresponded with where the energy was flowing into it. I've never experienced anything like it. It was like I was healing myself. Whether it was me or Warick, I don't know, but I didn't feel Warick's energy come over the top of mine like I felt previously when touching Ray and Max. I think it was my energy flowing into the cramping muscle. And I didn't intentionally will the energy to flow into the muscle. It just happened.

10 June 2021

Amazing! It's the middle of the night and I can't sleep, so I'm reading the book *DESTINY OF SOULS* by Michael Newton. I'm sure Warick intended me to purchase this book as another learning tool. I'm reading a section about the colours of spirits. A while ago, in this journal, I talked about seeing purple in my mind's eye, which I think is Warick. And more recently, through closed eyes, I saw my body glowing a beautiful, deep peacock blue colour. Newton says purple is the colour of highly evolved spirits called 'ascended masters' that don't seem to be incarnating. Blue is associated with spirits a level or two below purple. Newton talks about a halo—or white—that can be seen on the outer edge of the colour of the spirit. This could be the 'glowing' effect I saw around the blue colour on myself. I think I saw the colour of my spirit, which possibly makes me quite an evolved spirit. Newton said the halo colours represent attitudes, beliefs and unattained aspirations of the spirit. The vibrancy of white also indicates that a spirit can easily meld its vibrations with other spirits for clear communication. The character traits associated with purple are wisdom, truth and divinity; and for blue are knowledge, forgiveness and revelation. I find this incredible, that just a little while ago, for some reason I was able to see my spirit's colour with a glowing white halo at the edges—but with my eyes closed, and a short while later the subject, and what seems to be an explanation, appears in the book I'm reading. As I've said before, this happens way too often to be just a coincidence. There is no doubt in my mind that Warick and/or Elder are educating me while I'm conscious. But the question is why? Is it to help me understand why I'm here, what my life purpose is—to evolve my spirit through learnings in physical life? By knowing this, are they wanting to ensure I maximise my time here—this opportunity to learn as much as possible through life experiences? And through this experience and revelation and recording it in this journal, to then share it with you—the reader.

Am I able to help other people understand about the purpose of life, and help prove the existence of intelligent energy in the hope of humanity focusing on what's important in life—love? When my eyes are closed, I often see a pulsating, purple, circular shape, which I'm sure is Warick and possibly also Elder. I'm learning.

After reading about Spirit colours, I was still wide awake, so I decided to do a Joe Tracy meditation to open the third eye. I had an interesting experience. After following his suggestion to move your finger in a circular or swirling direction above your third eye, I felt a complete sense of peace come over me, like I know I'm in the zone with Warick or the spiritual dimension. It's a very distinct feeling. It's a pure uniform feeling, which seems to run through my core and possibly connect my chakras. In particular, I could feel this sensation connecting with my solar plexus area. During the meditation, this sensation occurred first, then I felt something external connect with me, or extend out from my root chakra. I have felt this often before and have described it in the journals. In one of Joe Tracy's meditations, he referred to it as something that connects you with tribe—that your root chakra enables you to connect with tribe. I've often wondered if the tingling sensations I get around my feet and legs are indicative of connecting with the spiritual dimension. I'm quite sure I have asked Warick about this using a pendulum, and at the time, he responded with, 'Yes'. While feeling peacefulness and the extension of energy from my root chakra during the meditation, I then felt a strong pressure at the top of the bridge of my nose. It was very strong and continued for about a minute, then receded. I have never experienced such a strong, distinct and localised pressure in this area before. I was sure that this must be it. Finally, my third eye was going to open, and that I would know it for sure. Unfortunately, the sensation came and went, as did the feeling of peace and extension of energy from my root chakra. It was over. I was a little disappointed. But I try to remain patient. The sensations I feel are very real. When I experience something as strong and distinct as the pressure at the top of the bridge of my nose, with my hands by my sides, it just reminds me that Spirit interaction with me is very real. No doubt. It's amazing and wonderful! Certainly nothing to be afraid of.

14 June 2021

It's important I write this down while I still remember, as I've been going on a journey lately with Joe Tracy's meditations, particularly those that leverage a past life to understand the purpose of your current life. I don't think I'm quite there yet. It's interesting that 'not quite there' feels like a life trait. Never quite there. Ballet as a little girl—selected among others for a special group who had the qualities our world-famous ballet teacher was looking for. I didn't practise and wasn't smart enough to learn the names of all the positions and movements. When my teacher was against my wanting to spend time playing sport instead of just focusing on ballet, I decided that was enough. I've never gone back to it, but I still remember the feeling of wearing pointe shoes and dancing on the tips of my toes. 'Not Quite There'. In high school, I struggled as a student. I had tutors for chemistry and English, and my Year 12 chemistry teacher told my parents that I wasn't university quality. I only just scraped through my Higher School Certificate, with a score of 282 out of 500. 'Not Quite There'. That said, I did find a university prepared to take me on that I really liked. And I did pass. I then did Honours at another university—the Australian National University in Canberra. I got second class Honours, ruling out the possibility of getting a scholarship to go on to do a PhD. 'Not Quite There'. After a year and a half of working as a technician and showing my bosses that I had a green thumb in the lab, they sponsored me, and I got a scholarship to do a PhD. After three and a half years, I finished but was found to be borderline. I had to sit before a panel of assessors to answer questions. 'Not Quite There'. It was the same in my science research career. I had plenty of passion, motivation and talent, but through other stories there were plenty of instances of 'Not Quite There'. During this time, I experienced a significant case of workplace bullying and sabotage of my research and lab that brought in the police and an investigation involving hidden cameras to detect what was happening.

I had to work in a locked lab as I received a negative letter where the words were made up of cutout letters pasted onto paper. All in all, 'Not Quite There'. I moved on to an amazing career in national security intelligence following the September 11 terrorist attacks on the US. My then husband was on one of the last flights out of the US after having flown across one of the attacked sites. The airlines told us nothing, and we didn't know if he was okay or one of the unlucky ones on a hijacked flight, until he landed in Australia. After five years, I tried a couple of avenues to progress my career in intelligence, but it was another case of 'Not Quite There', so I moved on. The next gig was being a CEO of a five-year national infrastructure program in the biosecurity sector. During this time, I studied at the Australian Institute of Company Directors, and in all honesty, I found some parts of it—like finance— very challenging. It was a case of 'Not Quite There', so I didn't finish the assessment needed for graduation. I also didn't find a way to secure enough funding to keep the infrastructure services we developed, going. So, it finished. 'Not Quite There' continued. It's been an interesting life to date. Despite the prevalence of 'Not Quite There', somehow I've managed to get from 'not university quality' to a PhD; an incredible experience in national security intelligence at a time of heightened global threat from terrorism; a CEO of a national infrastructure program; and what has now turned into fifteen years of leading complex and ambitious transformational change in cross-government, private and academic sectors. What was important to me—and continues to be important—is being able to earn a good income that enables me to do the things I want to do. Live life comfortably, have holidays and support my son through university until he gets a job and settles. Also, support an Indonesian family through this COVID crisis period, and sponsor their children through school to give them a good start in life. Since being CEO of the national infrastructure program, my career has meant less and less to me over time. There have certainly been things I've done that I'm very proud of during this time, but I can't help but feel like I'm killing time now. Much of the time I'd choose to do something else if given the choice. These days, no doubt about it, my passion lies in understanding, and wanting to develop, my ability to engage with Spirit. My dream now, if I'm so fortunate to have another dream come true after being able to live at Kianga, is for a publisher to fall in love with Warick's and my journey, that is recorded in these journals, and to feel as passionate as we do, and recognise the importance of getting this story out to the masses. In this regard, I'd love to be a famous writer with millions of copies of books sold, so I can stop doing what I don't really care about anymore and start doing what I love. I want to tell this story with Warick. I haven't been recording events that date back to 2013 for nothing.

I've taken a very long path tonight to land in a place to tell you about yet another 'Not Quite There' experience. Here we go. As recorded recently about the experiences I've had with Joe Tracy's past life regression meditations, I feel that I'm getting closer, and having insight, to what I was then and what I'm doing now. I feel that Warick is a protector and a loving companion, and Elder is my guide. A couple of nights ago, while doing a past life meditation to help understand your life's purpose, a few interesting things happened that shed some light on my current life. That said, it was another instance of 'Not Quite There'. When I opened the door to a past life, I stepped onto beautiful grass, and there was a thick mist. I knew I was back on the hilltop that adjoins the one with the ancient temple. Wolf was there to greet me and accompany me from the door to the temple. When I looked up at the temple, falcon was flying in the air and Warick was beckoning me to come. Next minute, Wolf took off towards him, and shortly after, I saw Wolf join Warick, who was waiting for me. When I arrived, I saw Elder looking out at the canyons. It was so lovely to see them all. I think they are my soul family. They are on this journey with me and have significant roles to play. We are a team. While standing with Elder and Warick looking at the canyons, I saw the most beautiful, large, white eagle gliding in the sky. I have no idea if there are white eagles and will have to Google this. It was so graceful and peaceful. It was very special. Like a sign. Picking up on my thoughts, Elder said to me, 'It's time. You're ready.' Next minute, Joe Tracy's guided meditation led me down some more steps to another door, which was in a side wall within the temple. It was a small narrow set of steps with a small wooden door. When I went through the door, I arrived in a small, dark place with a dimly lit set of stone stairs leading up to a large room. The room was like an ancient stone hall with high ceilings, a long table with ancient candelabra, and men seated on either side. It was a gathering. I saw Elder at the head of the table. They were there to discuss and consider me. My path. My purpose. They didn't open their mouths to speak; it was all telepathic. They were communicating with each other when I arrived. I could see their body language as they conversed with each other. They were wearing clothes like Elder wears. Very old fabrics and dull brown and fawn colours. Just before I was leaving, Elder said, 'Your purpose now, is to help others with their paths.' Use my wisdom and knowledge, intuition and perception to help them see and find their way. I felt a little disappointed in this as I thought my life purpose from this point would be more significant, particularly as it relates to this journal, and my journey with Warick and Elder. I thought to myself, 'I already help people in this way, so it's just more of the same', but maybe the difference now is I do this in a knowing, conscious way. Anyway, since then I've done another Joe Tracy meditation about miracles, so maybe I'll get lucky, and my miracle will come true. A publisher will want to publish Warick's and my story. I hope and pray so because that is where my heart and soul is now.

15 June 2021

It may not be anything, but it is worth noting. Tonight, at about 8.15 pm, there were two very clear knocks on a door that sounded like it came from downstairs. I was concerned that either Mum or her elder sister were trapped in a room, because the doorknobs throughout the house at Kianga keep coming off in your hand. Another thing to fix! The previous owners clearly put up with a lot of things that needed to be fixed. I decided I'd better go and check it out. They were sitting in the lounge watching TV and had heard it too. We all investigated and found nothing.

17 June 2021

It's just after midnight, and after been woken by Rosie barking outside the window, I'm now reading *DESTINY OF SOULS* by Michael Newton. Its content is proving to be very useful in validating what I experience with Warick, and possibly other Spirit energies. I've come to a section about how spirits are distinguished by colour, shape, energy resonance, and vibration. It also talks about the similarities of names of souls in a group. For instance, their names all starting with the same letter. I latched onto all of this as I've experienced tremendous diversity in what Warick can do with energy vibrations, and how I see what I call 'shadow shapes' of varying sizes and shapes. I remember Jane being the first to notice that John, Jules, Jane, and Joanne all start with the letter 'J', and Jules previously told me she has been a part of my circle. From the beginning, I've also felt a strong connection to John, where initially it felt like my soul was catching up with his long-lost friend. At times I think I've experienced his feelings without him telling me that something is wrong. It was so strong once, that it prompted me to ask him if something was wrong even though I didn't know him very well. This book has been wonderful so far in validating these things and educating me by providing information to inform my thinking about what it all means.

I've described it before, but the most common shadow shape I see floating closely around me, which is mostly in the right of my peripheral vision, is two dots with two lines. At times it seems cheeky, coming across in front of my vision to let me know it's there, and almost dancing up and down when we are at the beach, or we go for a walk at the lake. It sometimes also glides past me while I'm in the shower. It always fascinates me and is very real. It seems to have a personality and character of its own—the way it moves and behaves in different circumstances. I've also noticed sometimes its shape is crystal clear, while other times it's slightly out of focus, slightly blurry. Michael Newton's book DESTINY OF SOULS, also mentions pulsations of energy, which I have also often talked about in the journals. Warick, and possibly other guides, have done a good job guiding me to this book. The question in my mind now is, 'Why do they want me to consciously know all this stuff?' The book says colour, form, movement, and sound are individual markers of souls in their groups. There are resemblances of these elements between certain souls, and sound can be one of the most obvious, but the elements are also not uniform between group members.

22 June 2021

Every part of every page in the journal matters. A tree, a lumberjack, a factory that processes wood, a factory that processes paper, a journal production business, a sales company and store—all gave rise to the residual part of a piece of paper in this journal, that I've just written on. In this physical lifetime, in this moment, something will only occur once. The part of this page wasn't wasted, as can easily happen with my broad, sweeping pen strokes. It was appreciated, valued and reflected on. As should everything be.

Today, while driving to Kianga in the early morning, I killed a magpie. It hopped across the road in front of the car. In an attempt to do something to avoid the collision, I turned the steering wheel this way and that, and just like a man leading a lady in a dance, it responded this way and that, then it was over. I looked in the rear-view mirror, and feathers went everywhere. I prayed that it felt no pain entering death. In a prayer—one of the only ones I know—I asked for God's protection and love of the bird's soul that just passed. *'Eternal life grant unto thee oh Lord. May the perpetual light shine upon thee, and may thee rest in peace, Amen.'* My soul recognised its passing and the way I felt about it. I felt a strong surge of energy reach up from my solar plexus to my higher chakras, and energy tingling all over my back. I didn't want to end this bird, and I was so sorry for the fact that I had. The bird mattered in this life. I had no place interfering with its existence.

I'm recognising a few things coming together by way of Spirit colour, infinity and designing the covers of the first three *AWAKENING* books. I woke on Sunday morning with the idea to ask my neighbour if he would consider doing a piece of artwork for the covers of the first three books—my current journals. He agreed to meet with me later in the day. Over a glass of wine, I revealed to him my experience of Spirit and the journals. Apart from John, he is the only person outside of my immediate family who knows anything about it. It was a wonderful discussion. He didn't laugh at me or discard what I said, but instead related to it, sharing his own story of an aunt who experienced Spirit, and how he considers this in the world of art that he lives and breathes. No doubt Spirit put the idea in my mind. So why is this relevant to what is coming together? I learned my neighbour's passion is colour, where often his art only features colour. The way colour creates colour, and how created colour invokes something unique by way of emotion and expression. His art, I suspect, is unique in the world. A protégé of an elderly famous female artist in the UK. Based on our conversation, I shared with him the section in Michael Newton's book, *DESTINY OF SOULS*, about colours of Spirit, which I hope will stimulate and expand his thinking into new areas of creativity. He seems interested to create something for the book covers and has a lovely idea of interweaving stages of soul evolution from white to purple with the symbol of infinity. This would work well, where the second book is called *1NF1N1T1*, which connects the first and third books—like the symbol for infinity. At the same time, I also indicated that I'm happy for him to refer me to another artist if this is what he prefers. We shall see. ☺

23 June 2021

Things are still happening. Last night, I felt tingling at my root chakra, then a surge of energy moving up from this chakra, through my throat chakra and to the top of the bridge of my nose, where I also felt little movements. I then experienced a wave of heat come over my entire body, followed by a tone in my right ear, and Warick touching my right cheek. God only knows what Spirit—or spirits—were up to. I have no idea, but it was all very interesting. My conscious mind was acting like *Big Brother* video surveillance, aware of every single little thing that Spirit was doing. Something else in Michael Newton's book *DESTINY OF SOULS*, which I find really interesting, is he talks about how, shortly after souls pass over, they meet with a council of wise beings, which he calls 'Elders'. When I first met the elderly native American Indian male in a shamanic guided meditation by 'The Honest Guys', I immediately referred to him as Elder. This name just came to me. I didn't give any thought to it. Since this has all started, I've come to know that Elder is my guide, who mentors me and provides wise counsel. At times, he also tries to teach me things like how to use my energy. Warick on the other hand, protects and loves me. He is my Spirit companion through life. His energy often resides within my physical body. Coming across the elder counsel in the book, makes me wonder if Elder is a member of an elder council and is a wise being. It's possible when I see purple in my mind's eye that it is Elder. It may also be Warick.

29 June 2021

From time to time, I stop and reflect on what is commonly occurring around me by way of Spirit engagement. These days, I still see shadow shapes around me as I work, when I'm in the bathroom, when I drive, and when I go walking at the beach or lake. I think the shadow shapes are around me most of the time. They seem to get excited when I go for a walk to the beach in particular. It's like they tease me by bouncing in and out of my main field of view. I feel Warick in my face on and off during the day and night. He is very attuned to what I'm doing, paying more attention to some things than others. Like now, he is interested in what I'm writing. I feel his energy across my cheeks and cheekbones, and in my forehead where the third eye is located. I experience pressure on one side or the other of my face and ears, and on occasion I hear a tone. Sometimes I get the tone with no pressure. I associate this with a spirit visiting. Every night, Warick still communicates with me using pulse sounds. Last night, he took his time with this, and some pulse sounds were preceded by a strong feeling and sensation coming up from my solar plexus to my throat, and then to my forehead. I wish I understood what he is communicating to me. I still get physically hot when Spirit is engaging with me. Every day and night, I still feel the tingling energy around my feet, lower legs, and root and crown chakras. It's all wonderful and I wouldn't give any of this up for anything. I still hope and pray my abilities evolve. I can't hear spirits speaking to me, and I can't see apparitions of Spirit in human form. Warick does seem to be strongly focused on my third eye. Last night, I did a third eye activation meditation, which I haven't done for a while. I experienced a strong concentrated pressure in my third eye area for much of the meditation. I'll keep focusing on this for a while.

7 July 2021

It's really difficult to work out where to start in what I want to tell you. Jane, when we last got together, said she knew there was something substantial that I needed to work through with my job. Just like her knowing that Warick knew our circle would not meet on the morning when I became so sick, she also knew there was a significant problem with my path of work, and that I needed to deal with it before coming back to join the circle. At the time, my sickness was due to being so run down because of work worries. A short while later, I called it a day with the job and quit. Unfortunately, I jumped from the frying pan into the fire. I always wondered what it would be like to be a consultant. I attracted the attention of a little consultancy company wanting to break into the Canberra market and started working for them in early June. There was a reason for this step in my life. I knew it. But even before I started, I began to feel really uneasy about it. The partner in the company I was going to work for, started badgering me a week even before I started, dropping hints about putting in time to write a proposal to win work with government. They also wanted to know whether I knew people we could contract with certain skills to do work on another proposal. She reminded me so much of a woman I worked for years ago, who was the cause of a lot of misery in my life for about five years. An experience I never want to repeat again. No surprises, this is how my new boss turned out. I've been re-living the feelings caused by my previous boss's treatment where she made me feel highly inadequate. I knew she was often disappointed and frustrated with me. Although the experience toughened me up, and made me stronger, I don't ever want to go through it again. I've also realised over the past four weeks that I'm not cut out to be a full-on consultant, hungry to grow the business and proactively badger people to potentially give you work someday. I'm just not wired this way. I enjoy making a difference in people's lives by doing a good job, and I'm good at spotting opportunities and pursuing them to make as big a difference as possible. But that's it. I've only been in the job for four weeks and the feeling of unease, as though something is terribly wrong, has been growing every day to the point where today, I handed in my resignation. I just can't do it anymore. Even having a week to go until I finish, is almost too much to bear. This feeling is so strong. It's just like the times when I'm sure my intuition and soul drove me in certain directions. Its tangible and it doesn't stop until I make a change. Like when I left the national security intelligence sector to head up a national ICT infrastructure program for five years. Also, the two years that it took Ray and I to finally get together. It was the same feeling that drove me to resign, but the duration of this feeling was much shorter this time before I made a change. Maybe I'm learning to listen to my intuition and my soul. It's been a really tough twenty-four hours. Last night I tried to prepare Mum and Ray for my decision to resign. The concern of course is a financial one, where we are reliant on me pulling in a good income to carry my weight in financial affairs. Mum's response when I gave her a heads up was, 'That's sad.' In contrast, Ray's response was, 'Suck it up. Wait until you've secured another job.' Of course, that went down like a lead balloon. The response I hoped for from him was, 'It's your decision. Just know I'll be there to support you and stand by you no matter what.' Ray and I, despite the intuitive strong pull that brought us together, are now two people who love each other but are not intertwined. It's been an interesting week because a recent exchange with John suggests we have this in common. It's sad, but it's the way it is. It's life.

Despite all the anxiety and excruciating hesitation that I went through today, a wonderful thing did happen. Before submitting my resignation, I must have sat with my finger poised to hit the send button on the computer for at least half an hour. When I knew time was running out, as I had a meeting coming up with my boss, I sent it. As soon as I pressed the send button, I felt Warick touch my right cheek, letting me know he was there by my side, and that it's okay. It was completely unexpected and incredibly special. I love Warick so much for that. What he did, helped me so much. I've felt relieved and confident ever since. He knew how hard it was for me to do this. To resign when I don't even have another job to go to, or any prospects lined up.

The other really interesting thing that happened leading up to today, was last night when I couldn't sleep, I decided to do a meditation. While scrolling through a list of meditations that I'd saved, I accidently opened one by Joe Tracy called 'Sleep hypnosis for clearing negativity and building confidence'. I felt that Warick somehow intervened so this one would open. It's not one I would have chosen as I don't think I lack confidence. The meditation used a really interesting approach to get you to think about a time when you lacked confidence, and the occurrences that gave rise to it. At the beginning of the meditation, Joe got you to imagine yourself on a beach. For some reason, I saw myself as a tall and lanky, not so attractive, white Caucasian male in my fifties or sixties. I had blond hair. Not liking the scene and knowing I had a long way to go through the meditation, I tried to imagine myself as the native American Indian woman from Warick and Elder's time. It didn't work. I was brought back to the Caucasian man. I decided to go with it, thinking there must be something to it. I saw myself on a bus feeling complete despair and loneliness, numb from all that I experienced that wore me down and took away my confidence. It was horrible. I had flashes of my parents putting me down and making me feel unwanted, unloved and worthless all the time. Then being married to someone who did the same. I was never good enough, and this took away my confidence and sense of self to the point that it also impacted on my job and other work and family relationships. It was terrible. There was no end to it. Joe Tracy then got you to write in the sand on the beach all the things that took away your confidence and then got you to imagine the waves washing it all away. I did this. Then he got you to imagine the future at a time when things were different and you were full of confidence. The scene came to me easily. In the meditation, I calmly and confidently responded to a work call on a weekend from someone who needed to get my opinion on something. I said I'd talk to them further about it on Monday as my kids were waiting and wanting me to do something with them. I was completely comfortable in my skin. I was at peace and happy. It was wonderful. The interesting thing as Joe Tracy talked you down into a complete state of relaxation, is I felt Warick injecting a greater sense of relaxation a couple of times. Like he was wanting to make sure I was relaxed. After the meditation track finished, I reflected on what had just happened and why. What was the significance of this experience in the serious context of what has been happening in my work life? The penny dropped, and I started to see the parallels of what I think I experienced in a former life as a white Caucasian male with what is occurring in my current life. Flashing through my mind were all the occasions I've experienced where my confidence has been downtrodden, starting from when I was a child. I've never even realised this before, that this has continued to happen through my entire life, and in very significant and serious ways. As a little ballerina of less than ten years old, being singled out on numerous occasions by my ballet teacher, in front of the entire class, for being inadequate. As a primary school student, not very pretty or smart, being picked on by other students to the point where I hated school and wanted to leave. At high school, my chemistry teacher telling my parents that I was not university quality. When I was engaged during university, and my fiancé's mother saying my time would be better spent not going to university, but rather working in a bank to save money for when we got married. My Honours supervisor, not thinking highly of me and thinking I'm only capable of being a lab technician. My husband, who spent years listing and telling me all the things that he didn't like about me, which ended in a domestic abuse situation, where I no longer felt like I had an identity. In a post-doctoral job, being the subject of workplace bullying from my boss, that ended with a police investigation and the deputy vice chancellor of the university saying to me, 'You have walked through the valley of hell. Just keep on walking.' Experiencing other workplace mistreatment situations, including the boss I mentioned earlier—a male boss in a security intelligence organisation—and now in the job I just resigned from. All these significant episodes flashed through my mind one after another. I wondered why. It became clear to me that my life has been full of occasions where my confidence has been knocked. At the end of five years working for the woman I mentioned earlier, I had been numb on so many occasions that I toughened up. This is where my real confidence that was always within me, finally came out good and strong. I have often said to people, 'The number of times my old boss gave me a compliment in the five years I worked for her, I can count on one hand.' I also described the way I felt on those occasions was like 'being a dog in a metal trash can with the lid on, and her banging the hell out of it with a stick'. It was one of the worst times in my life. So why did I need to become aware of this lesson now? I realised part of the purpose of this life is to learn this lesson. Maybe the lesson is, *Always believe in yourself, and don't let others make you question yourself or have self-doubt. Don't stop loving yourself. Also, don't stand for mistreatment. Get out of the situation no matter how difficult. It's not worth it. Your love of self is more important than putting up with people that just want to bring you down, whether consciously or subconsciously. Believe in yourself. You have value. Go where this value can be loved and realised. Don't allow your positive energy to be changed into negative energy. You can't be all you can be, and make a difference to others, if you lose your confidence and sense of self and value.* Well, today I didn't put up with it. I didn't let it pull me down. I pulled the pin. And I felt relieved and happy that I did. Mind you, I haven't had the courage to tell Ray yet given his response to the idea that I wanted to resign. It will come out at some stage, just not today. Today has been enough to cope with. ☺

8 July 2021

And today just got worse. The small company I just handed my resignation to, asked me to, in my remaining days, develop a tool for them based on what I do best—setting up and restoring large and complex transformation programs. Unbelievable! As my boss was speaking, I thought to myself, *So you want me to give you my intellectual property*. And of course, I didn't say anything there and then! I was just my usual obliging self. Shortly after the call, my blood began to boil. Within ten minutes, I sent her an email saying I wasn't comfortable doing this as essentially I'd be handing over my intellectual property. I asked if I could finish with the company today, and later, in a brief call, she agreed. What you generate while working for an organisation becomes their intellectual property. I wouldn't have just been giving them my intellectual property but also ruling out my ability to use it myself. How stupid do they think I am? That all said, a lovely thing did happen last night. I woke to feel Warick's energy vibrating on the outside of my body as he started to blend and merge with me. It woke me. His energy was over my entire body. I haven't felt him do this for a while. It was really special. Occasionally, I let him know that I miss this kind of external stimulation. I hope from time to time he continues to do it.

9 July 2021

I'm not upset with my decision to leave the small consultancy company. I'm confident and proud that I did. Proud that I didn't let my boss take advantage of me by happily handing over my intellectual property. There is no exaggeration that it is intellectual property. I've been successfully leading change and transformation in challenging complex stakeholder environments for more than 17 years. Whether I'm setting them up for success, or getting them back on track, I have a knack at doing it. And I'm passionate about it. It's one of the things I'm known for across the public sector. I'm also a nice and humble person who doesn't like confrontation. I'm also quite intelligent and feel what people are thinking. Warick just touched my right check agreeing with this. Because I feel what people think, I tend to internalise their emotions. I'm not good at blocking this from happening. When I'm around angry, frustrated, disappointed people, I feel everything they are feeling. It really brings me down. So much so, it can make me physically sick. For the past four weeks, I've felt every instance of my boss's emotions of disappointment and frustration with me. She's a highly driven and intelligent person, so I suspect she tends to have high expectations, pushes, and is demanding of those around her. In the first conversation I had with the business manager of the company, she told me, 'You are going to have to push back on the boss; she is very impatient and demanding.' My boss even told me she's very impatient. It's interesting that in a later conversation with the business manager, when she was explaining to me about a health condition she has, it was clear that although the staff of the company know they need to push back at the boss, they don't do it very well. Why am I talking about these things? Because it's important. They are all lessons. The right choice was to leave, not to stay. When I worked for someone like this in the past, what happens over time when you know they are disappointed in you, is it chews away at your self-confidence and makes you question yourself.

It's so important to spot this happening early and leave—and no longer associate with the person. The other thing I've learned from this came from them wanting me to give away my intellectual property. First, I experienced anger and thought, 'Do they think I'm stupid?' Sleeping on it, and reflecting on it further, it tells me that my boss thinks her intelligence is superior by thinking she might get away with asking me in a very nice way, from an angle of, 'This is something you might enjoy doing.' I was not prepared for what she said. Why? Because I trusted her. She essentially used her 'superior intelligence' and took advantage of the trust she had established with me. I suspect she does this a lot to get what she wants. It's horrible. I didn't respond in the moment, but I'm very glad I did shortly after. The pressure is now on to find another job as I have a finite amount of savings to get me through. Based on previous occasions, it can take me around three months to identify something suitable. I hope it takes no more than half this time.

11 July 2021

I'm hesitant to write about this topic, but it doesn't seem right for me to bare my soul on some subjects and not others. There are also personal relationships to consider, plus the thought if I don't write about it, I may not make the connection to something significant later. I see shadow shapes around my hand as I'm writing this, and I suspect Warick is close by. It's possible that Warick is who I'm seeing. A few things have come up lately that seem, or should I say *feel*, intertwined. On occasion, something that occurs in the present links to something I've written about in an earlier journal. It comes to my attention at just the right time when I'm typing up a section from an earlier journal on the computer. I realise it has relevance to what is occurring in the present moment. I hope this makes sense. This series of events involve what I typed up from my second journal called AWAKENING II - 1NF1N1T1, John's response to reading it, and a section I read recently in the book called, *Destiny of Souls*—and in that order. It's a matter of the heart and love for your partner, husband or wife. In an entry I recently typed up from the AWAKENING II - 1NF1N1T1 journal, I made an observation about John's reaction to what I wrote. It's interesting because in his response, he was selective in what he responded to. I concluded that his conscious mind guards and protects him and keeps me at arm's length. In the journal 1NF1N1T1, I wanted to leave a message for him in the hope that one day he might read it, basically letting him know that I know he does this and that it is okay. As usual, I sent John the latest section of the journal that I'd typed up, which contained this message to him. It made him think. What was nice is, he opened up for a change and talked about his relationships with women and said how he has always been guarded. He said he doesn't have deep love. I think to some extent this is because of his closed nature. What's interesting is, last night I read a section in *Destiny of Souls* that talks about the types of relationships between souls. The term 'deep love' came up again in the context of the type of love that exists between 'primary soulmates'. In response to John's openness, I provided some insight to my own experiences with love, and that I too am the type who walks through life on my own, despite the relationships around me. John described it as 'his universe'. I have a saying that comes out from time to time: 'You came into this world on your own, and you'll go out on your own.' It's how I feel, and how I tend to live my life. It doesn't seem to matter who I'm with; sooner or later I seem to distance myself. I go back to walking my own path. This has been the result with every romantic relationship I've had. I'm not able to keep the 'deep love' going. I don't know why. I've concluded I'm probably not a good mate to have in that sense. I'm so independent and very happy in my own company. In fact, I need my own time. There must be a learning in this for me. Something I'm supposed to learn in my life. I don't like to hurt people. I hope I never do again. I tossed and turned over this one last night. I've wondered if Warick is my 'primary soulmate'. I suspect he is. In some ways, it feels like a test. He won't give me a straight answer when I've asked him about this lately. I'm glad John opened up to me about this, and I'm glad we seem to share the same 'problem'. I'm also glad I've now written about it in the journal as it may become significant down the track. We shall see.

13 July 2021

I'm really glad I've read a section of Michael Newton's book, *DESTINY OF SOULS*, about soul 'community dynamics'. In particular, what a primary soulmate is, a companion soulmate and an affiliated soulmate. The primary soulmate is a closely bonded partner. No other soul is more important to you, and they enrich your existence beyond measure. A great motivator for souls to incarnate is the opportunity for expression in physical form. This is attractive particularly to primary soulmates. They can be your spouse, brother, sister, or best friend, or occasionally a parent. You can also change genders between lifetimes, but usually souls choose one gender over another about 75% of the time. The book says our primary soulmate is our eternal partner. I find this interesting because I consider Warick to be an eternal love that has lasted through the ages, and has now come back to me, across dimensions, with a big bang. We now exist together in Spirit and physical form on Earth. Elder has also referred to his relationship with me as 'eternal'. I wonder, for this journal, whether I should call it *Eternal Love*. Michael Newton's book *DESTINY OF SOULS* talks about other souls in our primary cluster group who can be called soulmates. Michael Newton refers to them as 'soul companions'. They have differences in character, and a variety of talents that complement each other. Within the cluster group, there is usually an inner circle of souls who are especially close to you, who play important support roles in your lives, and you do the same for them. The inner circle started their existence together but have different rates of development. Michael Newton also talked about 'affiliated souls' who are members of secondary groups outside of your primary cluster group but are in the same general spiritual vicinity. This can be up to 1,000 souls or more, whereas you usually have only three to five souls in your companion soulmate inner circle. There are certain affiliated souls in other groups who are selected to work with you and whom you come to know over many lives, while others may cross our path only briefly. Often our parents come from a nearby cluster group. So apart from being interesting, why does this all matter? Because I often wonder about the connections I have with Ray, John and Warrick. Ray and I certainly experienced a 'deep love' for several years when we first got together. In fact, it was so strong that over a period of two years, no matter how hard each of us tried, we couldn't let each other go. It was complicated, involving other people, which I won't go into here. During my life, I have repeatedly drifted back to my 'sole' existence when I'm with someone. I don't necessarily want to leave them, but I'm happy to walk my own path in my own company much of the time. I don't know why. I suspect I'm not learning whatever lesson I'm supposed to learn here, which is why it seems to always happen. I love Ray very much and won't let him down, but I have largely reverted to walking my own path, where I often seek solitude. The nature of my connection to John has also been something I've wondered about, especially because when we first connected, I experienced a very strong feeling towards him, which came from my solar plexus—a soul connection of some sort. A feeling like what I've experienced in the past, when my intuition has strongly pushed me in a certain direction, no matter what I thought at the time. When this happens, it's unrelenting and very strong. I felt this when I left the national security intelligence community to become a CEO of a national ICT infrastructure program; when I met Ray; when I met John; and now, just recently, in association with wanting to leave my job with the small consultancy company. Last night, I used the pendulum to ask Warick about what type of soul connection I have with himself, Ray and John. As usual, Warick was not interested in using the pendulum and immediately started to touch my cheeks to provide a response to my questions. Through persistence, I did manage to get answers through use of the pendulum, which was useful because he didn't provide a cheek response to all questions. Essentially, he confirmed that he is my primary soulmate, John is a companion soulmate, and Ray is an affiliate soul. To be honest, how I feel now agrees with this. Despite the strong bond I have with Ray, I suspect that he and I are together to help each other learn. We certainly do test each other at times. When I first met Ray, he led with his head and not his heart. When he gave in and came to me for good, he came with his heart. Maybe he learned love is what is most important. I have so much to be thankful for with Ray. Importantly, I wouldn't be all that I am today, and achieved all that I have achieved, without the fact he just loved me for who I am. He accepted all that I am, and supported me, no matter what. Despite some initial flare ups within him, his heart always ended up leading, and he usually supports me even if he doesn't agree with me. The person I was married to, was the absolute opposite. His attitude towards me, chewed away at me for years, gradually removing all sense of self, until I eventually left. Ray's ability to lead with his heart, and what this has meant by way of support to me, I would have to say has been the most important thing about this relationship.

I want to conclude this entry by saying how reading about the nature of connections between souls has helped me. As I said in the first journal, when Warick first came to me, I could love both Ray and Warick because one is human, and one is Spirit. I've learned through Michael's book, *DESTINY OF SOULS*, that what gender you are, and the relationship you have, between souls, changes between lifetimes. That your spouse is not always your primary soulmate, and that's okay because there are lessons you are learning with someone else. Also, that you can love all these different connected souls in intimate and other ways. I feel a lot more comfortable now about the feelings I have towards Ray, John and Warick. They make sense, and I feel like I don't need to dance around this subject anymore. It's wonderful that, at the end of the day, it's about the care we have for each other, and how we are trying to help each other learn. I wonder if Michael Newton ever came across a case of a primary soulmate, who did not incarnate with a person in a particular physical lifetime, but instead, came across the spiritual divide to be with them. For the physical person, the mind has no memory of the relationship. For Warick and I, as John has said, it's amazing all the different ways Warick expresses love for me, without being able to say a word.

14 July 2021

Across the world, four million people are now dead from COVID, and that's an official record. I'm sure there are many others that aren't recorded. Countries that are rolling out the vaccine fast, are stepping towards normal living. There are many countries, including ours, that are still impacted. For us, it's a case of weighing up the fear of a vaccine possibly taking your life due to blood clots, versus a low risk of catching COVID because we have managed to keep it mostly under wraps. But, how quickly the tables can turn with Sydney now having four hundred active cases, and seven thousand close contacts. Our hearts go out to the family we support in Indonesia where, on average, there are one thousand deaths per day, mass graves and use of a vaccine, which is proving to not be very effective.

During the night, Warick is still merging with me, sometimes to a stage where I feel a sense of peace. He's also making the usual pulse sounds, which is really lovely. Last night, I also felt Warick's vibration outside of my body. I could feel it with my hand for a while on the bed, and in front of my face and behind my head. I love being able to experience his energy in different ways. He is touching my right cheek now in agreement with this.

You may remember me talking about Wolf, a spirit wolf, who I call 'Wolf', which I encountered initially during a guided meditation. It unexpectedly came out onto a path that I was walking on through a forest. Wolf has medium-length hair, with grey flecks and dark features around its face. It has a long nose, and always appears to have its head down slightly, with eyes glancing up at me, giving a piercing look that holds my attention. It's like Wolf is looking straight through me. It has a beautiful thick, soft coat.

Wolf has been appearing in my meditations on and off for quite some time now, when I visit Warick and Elder. I sense that we are deeply connected. I know this sounds strange, but I sometimes miss Wolf. We have this mutual respect. I know he's dangerous and wild, but he always stays with me and protects me. Sometimes, he also protects Warick, but I may be wrong about this because the time I'm recalling as I'm writing this entry, was the time I found myself in Warick's body on a hunting expedition with other men. I wrote this up in the journal at the time. I think Wolf sensed it was my consciousness in Warick's body, and that's why he was trailing behind following us in the forest. I assumed Wolf is an animal spirit guide. Last night, I searched on *YouTube* about wolf spirit guides. I found one informative video, which I thought was quite good. It was called *The Wolf Spirit – Spiritual Animal Symbolism* by Healing Elements. It talked about your qualities if you have a wolf spirit connection, or guide. I thought it was worth listing the qualities as I think it's pretty spot-on in describing who I am, and probably also goes a long way to explaining why I always revert to walking my own path. I suspect Warick led me to wondering about Wolf and wanting me to research it so I would better understand myself. Who I am. It's incredible how he can place a thought in my mind and lead me somewhere. It's obvious when he does this. It's like some random thought that just comes to mind without any associated context that I'm conscious about. Here is the list of qualities:

- Instinctive animal – uses gut feelings to make decisions.
- Very diverse abilities – able to work effectively with others and yourself.
- People respond to you, and you can harness their collective offerings.
- Can pull away from the pack, be alone, and accomplish success on your own.
- On guard – don't fully trust – observe situations for red flags.
- Intelligent, strategic, calculated, and plan your path. Focus on the next step in your life. Have a driving force to execute the next step.
- Use instincts well. Your intuition never steers you wrong. Correct in trusting your instincts. It leads you to safety. Can tap into the wisdom of ancestors through dreams.
- You blend mindfulness with emotional mindset.
- Have extreme raw emotions. You backup your emotions with bite.
- Defend your pack, those you love. Sacrifice own life to save another you love.
- So strong – can put your instinctive thoughts onto others. Need to not be too influential to allow others to learn.
- You have a fundamental need for freedom. You hate suffocation and people asking you to follow the crowd. You're a leader. Will break through anything that holds you down.
- Very hardy – have endurance to go through challenges without complaining, which is something that draws people to you.
- You need to always express your authentic self. You don't hold back your opinions. You need to be honest. Live with integrity. You believe in being brutely honest.
- Very magical when you follow your integrity and intuition. Can manifest extremely positive outcomes that seem out of a dream. Can follow the law of attraction, be grateful for what you have, and through hard work, can manifest extremely positive outcomes and sustainability.
- You prefer ritual – structured living and you like ceremony, like native American Indian and other cultures.

- You live by moral codes and value these. It is one of the most important factors that makes you, you.
- Have wisdom and can provide guidance to be a fierce leader and can provide assurance to others. Have loyal qualities.
- You know thyself – heart, mind and soul.

No doubt about it. I have most of these qualities and this does help me understand why I always revert to walking my own path, and I need solitude and freedom. It also explains how others perceive me, and why I seem to have this magic ability in bringing people together to work effectively. This is something I'm known for in my line of work. A friend of ours is a deep thinker, and I'm strongly connected to him. He summed me up one day, saying how people are drawn to me and look to me for leadership. This is true, and it happens with my family, friends and in work situations. Not with John though, which I like. It's hard to explain, but from my perspective it's like John and I look straight into each other's eyes on the same wavelength. There's nothing between us—just honesty. Sharing moments, thoughts and experiences in our lives, that are occurring on opposite sides of the planet. It's interesting, and I like knowing he's there. It's a good relationship to have.

I suppose what's most special about Warick helping me to understand why I am the way I am, in walking my own path for instance, is that it tells me it's okay, there is nothing wrong with me. It's just who I am, and these are a part of the qualities I have. I've always loved dogs. I think between this, Wolf's spirit coming into my life through meditation, and my strong alignment with the qualities of a wolf—which is a pretty spot-on description of who I am—I feel more at ease, and comfortable with who I am. Thanks Warick.

15 July 2021

It was an interesting morning, as I woke to Warick's energy already spread throughout my body. Even when I moved, he was still there. As I lay still, I felt Warick's energy taking over, and he moved my head slowly a few times. I felt the tingling, prickly energy sensation in my feet, hands and root chakra that I usually feel when connected to the spirit realm. The most obvious feeling, however, was Warick's energy spread throughout my body. I get the feeling he's still working with me towards possible trance mediumship, where he takes over my body and can talk through me. Either that, or he just likes hanging out in my body. A few times I experienced what seemed like flashes of my conscious self being slightly to the right of my physical self. Not far away, but immediately next to my head. I was still fully conscious at the time but dislodged from my head for a split second. It was an interesting sensation. I felt perfectly fine when it happened. It was incredibly fast. It happened; I made a mental note that it did; and then I was consciously back in place within my head. Also, a few times I experienced flashes of black outs. It was just as fast, but when this happened, I knew I had gone for a split second and had no memory of the split second. Completely blank, as though I was asleep. I wonder if Warick is starting to experiment with putting my mind aside and getting me used to the sensations. I think I like the 'being conscious' option better, so I don't miss anything.

Questions to Warick using the pendulum:

- Will a publisher that I've already sent the manuscript to want to publish it? Yes
- Will the *AWAKENING* series find a way to be communicated to the world at some stage during or after my life? Yes

- Does the spirit world, the source and higher-level beings, want to see the *AWAKENING* series be communicated to the world? Yes
- Was writing the *AWAKENING* series a part of my life plan? Yes
- Am I supposed to help humanity with this? Yes

17 July 2021

More than twelve million people in Australia go into lockdown as the Delta variant, a rapid spreader of COVID, moves through the states of New South Wales and Victoria. In one day in Indonesia, a thousand deaths and fifty-three thousand newly detected cases, surpassing India's record of newly detected cases in a day. The world is far from normal. It will be quite some time before the world opens up the way it was.

Early this morning, it was interesting. When expressing love to Warick, instead of just thinking the words in my mind, I on purpose drew upwards through my chakras a wave of energy that was my feeling of love. I remember in my mind, focusing and trying to pull up my emotion of love, to then portray it up and out of my head towards Warick. It was quite intense, and not an easy thing to do, but I did it. I asked him if he felt that, and he is touching my right cheek now confirming that he did. It lasted maybe ten seconds, and I had to keep concentrating and willing my emotions and feelings up through my chakras. By the end, I could feel sensations at my root chakra and in my throat and forehead, so I know I was connected. Lately, it's been bothering me that when I tell Warick I love him, that it is just words. I'm sure a couple of times I've managed portraying some feeling of emotion, but today it was very clear that I did, and that it was me and not Warick using emotional energy to communicate. Pretty amazing, and definitely something I need to practise. It's incredible that after all I've experienced, there are still new things that happen. I know I don't experience all the things that mediums and psychics say they do. In this lifetime, I hope I do, but I'm appreciative of all that I do experience. Apart from recording the events in this journal, sharing my journey with John, and loving Warick, I don't know if there will be any more to it. I hope so, but even if not, I'm lucky to have John and Warick in my life.

18 July 2022

I'm tired this morning. The last two nights I've been very restless and wide awake, particularly around three to four in the morning. Last night, while not sleeping, I read some more of *DESTINY OF SOULS*. There are a few things that have resonated with me that are worth recording as they validate and help to explain what I've experienced. For simplicity, I'll list them with my associated thoughts.

- Michael Newton talks about intimate relations between spirits. He said, 'Love is a desire for full unification with the object of that love' and '…. erotic power of two minds that are completely joined', and 'a major incentive for many souls to reincarnate, is the pleasures of physical expression in biological form'. I've said quite a lot about Warick's intimate encounters with me, which occurred earlier on and then became less frequent. The first encounters were like he—or in my mind, still the possibility of it being a different spirit because the energy was so strong and rapid, I could barely stand it —was trying to behave like a human would, and stimulate me, and interact with me like a man would. He did a diversity of things. It amazed me how his energy could stimulate areas inside my body, far beyond what any physical man could do. This does make me wonder whether it was Warick wanting me to love and trust him, possibly another spirit, or as Michael Newton said, possibly a spirit visiting Earth on what he calls 'recreation time', getting up to things maybe it shouldn't, in memory of what it was like to be human and be intimate with a woman. When these initial intense intimate interactions subsided, Warick periodically merged his energy with mine, where we would reach a state of having a complete sense of peace, where I could no longer feel my body. While in this state, Warick would pulse his energy through us, which was really stimulating all over, in a very intimate way. I'd say it was like what a woman feels when she orgasms, but the sensation runs through your entire body. In our case, it moved through our merged energies. Michael Newton's words about complete unification with the object of your love by two minds combining, validates in my mind what Warick was doing when we merged completely in this way. I've noticed that Warick still merges with me quite a lot, but not quite like what I have just described. Our energies merge, but without reaching the complete sense of peace. I don't know whether he's just wanting to be close to me, or if he's working towards being able to do something with me. He is touching my right cheek now, so I suspect it is the latter.

- In Michael Newton's book, he includes a recollection from a client describing how souls engage in dance, music and games, for recreation. A client said, 'They move in a circle, faster and faster, until they look like a whirlwind with no space between them. A cascading turbulence, which is a joining of souls.' At the end of this dance, the client describes them as having 'experienced the intricate differences between their vibrational energy patterns'. To me, this also validates the experiences I've had with Warick merging his energy with mine. It validates that souls do this as a means of experiencing, and better understanding, each other. It's possible one of the reasons why Warick does this with me, is to get to know the intricacies of my vibrational energy patterns. It may help him better interact with me and possibly work with me to enable us to one day do certain things together. I don't know. Either that, or he just does it because he loves me and wants to be close to my soul.
- Lastly, Michael Newton talks about 'musical thought being the language of souls. The composition and transmission of harmonic resonance appears to relate to the formation and presentation of spiritual language'. I've always wondered about the tones that I experience, with what I describe as 'incoming Spirit'. Kerry McLeod from My Mediumship said this is Spirit trying to tune in with my frequency, like a radio. What Michael talks about, by way of music being the language of souls, validates in my mind that the tone I hear when a spirit drops in, is their attempt to communicate with me as are the times when Warick does what I describe as 'pulse sound language'. I really

wish my soul would let my conscious brain know what they are saying. It's possible I'm just not fully wired up yet between my chakras to enable this. I remember Phil from My Mediumship saying something about how you take in spirit communication through your throat to your brain. Something like this. I need to check my notes that I made when he said this. I definitely feel more in my throat chakra area these days, so maybe it just isn't connected yet with what I need to be able to understand about what spirits are saying when they make these tone and pulse sounds. It's all really interesting, and I hope my abilities continue to evolve in this regard.

Something else that's worth noting in this entry is, this morning, while asking Warick questions with the pendulum, I could feel pressure in my throat pushing up to the back and roof of my mouth, and across my cheeks and to my forehead. When I made this note in the journal, where I record outcomes from using the pendulum, Warick touched my right cheek agreeing with me.

Questions to Warick using the pendulum:

- Will my psychic and medium abilities continue to evolve in this lifetime? Yes
- Will I use my psychic and medium abilities? Yes
- Will a publisher I've already sent the manuscript to want to publish it? Yes
- Warick, did you feel my love emotion that I portrayed to you yesterday morning? Yes
- Is my hair colour blue? No

20 July 2021

A brief entry while watching a TV show called *Insiders* on ABC. This occurred when I was on my own at home on Sunday at Kianga, on 18 July. While sitting on the couch, I heard a very distinct and quite loud movement of papers close to me on my left side. It sounded just like someone pulling a piece of paper out from among other papers. This was around nine thirty in the morning. The sound was unmistakable and could not be due to another cause. Nothing was there.

21 July 2021

It's been an interesting day. After spending some time with Warick, Elder and Wolf in meditation, which calmed and reassured me, I've just completed a past life regression session with Brian Weiss using a recorded session on *YouTube* called 'Past Life Regression Session'. It was fantastic, despite having occasional commercials, which I needed to ignore to maintain focus. With ease, I remembered a childhood scene, starting with a favourite doll and then moving onto a series of scenes with my grandmother, Nanna Banyer. At the end of the memories, Brian asked, 'Why would you remember these scenes?' As I realised many of my early (less than three years old) memories were with my, Nanna Banyer, I experienced a really strong tingling energy on the entire underside of my body, which got stronger as I thought of her. I'm sure she was visiting me and that what I experienced was her energy. I need to remember this type of energy in case she visits again. It was a strong tingling energy that got stronger. It's really different to Warick's energy. It was wonderful!

The last couple of nights I've been seeing 4:44 and 3:33. I looked up their meaning on *YouTube*. Numerology Nation says *333 is a sign of growth and to eliminate the things that make you unhappy. It also says to keep working on all that you desire as spiritual growth. Guides and angels will provide you with support and encouragement. Be centred and balanced.* This is interesting because when I met up with Elder during meditation today, he asked me to look out beyond the cliffs where we were standing and tell him what I saw. I said nature, peace, harmony, balance. He said I need to ensure I have balance across all aspects of my life. Love is what is most important. I need to be all that I am to everyone, and everything, in all aspects of my life. Numerology Nation says 444 means *love and encouragement from guides and angels. If struggling and floundering, they are encouraging you to take action and are there to help. I just need to ask. I have full support to take action. Change is ahead.*

22 July 2021

When I checked my emails this morning, I noticed a person from a recruitment agency had sent me a message at 11:11 pm. There certainly is quite a lot of Spirit and Angel activity around me at the moment, which I really appreciate and find comforting at this time when there is uncertainty about my job and what will become of the *AWAKENING* series—something that has become increasingly important to me. Yesterday, I sent the manuscript to another eleven publishers. A couple were ones I came across in the Blue Kingdom metaphysical shop in Braidwood, which is a small village between Canberra and the South Coast of New South Wales. I also found a really good list of the top nineteen publishers of metaphysical books online. Although dated, this proved to be useful. Last night was really interesting. I woke to feel a spirit entering and fully occupying my entire face. It felt like it was a bit big for the size of my face as I could also feel its energy like a halo around the edges. In my mind, I asked if it was Warick, but I got no response. Instead, it made my lips squeeze together like you would do if you're about to give someone a kiss. It did this numerous times and made my face smile slightly. I think it may have been a different spirit to Warick. I wondered if it was my Nanna Banyer. I don't know. While this was happening, I also felt a strong feeling up through my root chakra and my left lower calf muscle. This went on for about fifteen minutes or so. Shortly afterwards, I heard two voices in quick succession. The first said, 'Hello' with a rising pitch as the word was said. It was an English accent. Then a second voice, from a different source, said two words, which I can't remember. It wasn't significant and just like casual conversation. This was also an English accent. Both voices were male. The voices were very clear—and close—as though they were sparking up a conversation with me in a friendly and casual way. It was terrific! Maybe this is a breakthrough on being able to hear

Spirit. After this, I heard what sounded like a single brief tone in my right ear, just like the one I hear when I put in my ear buds. I've heard this numerous times over the past week or so, during the night and especially when I roll onto my side and my head moves on the pillow. I'm not sure what to make of it. I certainly don't have my ear buds in. It's strange.

23 July 2021

I'm not well. A week ago, my mother became very ill with a virus and chest infection. Her symptoms started with extreme weakness, body aches and pains and the inability to get warm. I looked after her during this time, and now a week later, I've got the same symptoms of extreme lethargy, tiredness and body aches. Last night while in bed, I couldn't get warm. I took some painkillers and after about half an hour, they started to kick in. In my mind, I asked Warick, Elder and other spirits if they could help me by using their healing energy and love. In response, Warick touched my right cheek. I then felt a wave of energy spreading out across my body, starting in the middle of my back. It felt lovely and I knew this was Warick—and possibly other spirits—trying to heal me. It lasted a couple of minutes. I thanked them. I'm so appreciative of their willingness and ability to heal me. Shortly after, I managed to get off to sleep. When I woke this morning, I didn't feel too bad, so I started shifting soil for a new vegetable garden at Kianga. By late morning, I had to stop as symptoms set in again. I slept for a couple of hours this afternoon. I hope tonight Warick spends time healing me again. I could really do with his help.

24 July 2021

The synchronicity of numbers continues. I am seeing 3:11 on my phone through the night. This morning while lying on the couch—as I'm so unwell—I listened to a couple of *YouTube* videos on the meaning of 311 and 11:11. When I closed the cover on my phone, I noticed the time was 11:11. After having a sleep, I listened to another description of the meaning of 11:11 by Your Youniverse, called '1111 Meaning: Why you keep seeing '1111' and '11:11' (and how to use it)'. The introduction and referrals to other material at the beginning is a bit annoying, but hang in there, because the information particularly towards the end is good. I've written about 11:11 before, at a time when John and I were experiencing a string of shared synchronicities. It makes me wonder with him being in Alaska on holidays, and out of range, whether he is experiencing any of these things now. Seeing 11:11 repeatedly again, is making me reflect on its meaning and my current mindset and circumstances. 11:11 indicates new beginnings and awakening. Your thoughts are manifesting your reality. What has mostly been in my mind lately, is a strong desire for the first journal *AWAKENING – The Beginning* to be published. I've now submitted it to another eleven publishers. Unfortunately, my neighbour, who is an artist specialising in colour, has lost interest in doing a piece of artwork for the book cover. Recently, I came across another artist who seems to specialise in abstract colour paintings. I first saw one of her paintings while having a video linkup with a recruitment agent for a completely different reason. It was hanging behind her. I was lucky, because the recruitment agent was happy to share the contact details of the artist. I've reached out to the artist, and she is happy to do a commissioned piece of work for my book. Interestingly, the name of the painting that hung behind the recruitment agent had 'Mermaid' in it—something which I think I'm spiritually connected to, but I don't know why. I also chased up Jane about the name of the spirit medium artist who sketches people's spirit guides and loved ones who have passed. Once I'm working again and have the money, I'll commission some work from both of them. I'm a little nervous about the spirit artist because in my mind I have an image of what Warick and Elder look like from my meditations with them. It will be interesting to see what she comes up with. Also prominent in my mind at the moment, is my job situation. Although the thought of project contract work is not what my heart and soul want to do, I do respect that the financial element is critical for my happiness, including my ability to support those I love. Ideally, it would be great if I could secure a role that pays well enough for me to work four days a week and work from home one day a week. This would enable me to spend more time doing the things I love. Hopefully seeing 11:11 repeatedly, and other number sequences, means I'm on the right path and that these things will fall into place. Today, I've had absolutely no energy and have been struggling to keep my eyes open. I ended up back in bed for the afternoon. I've noticed a lot of shadow shape activity around me. It's lovely to know they are there, and they care.

25 July 2021

I'm starting to be on the mend now. I've decided to take it easy again today, however, as I still feel very tired. I spent some time at the beach with the dogs. It was lovely. A beautiful day—calm seas. Perfect for sitting on the sand and watching people body surf in the middle of winter! After lunch, I decided to do some relaxation meditation with the possibility of falling asleep. I was too tired to try a Joe Tracy past life regression, so I decided on some healing meditation music instead. In my mind, I reached out to Warick to see if he had a preference, but he provided no response. I played a meditation track called 'Reiki Zen Aura Healing Meditation Music Positive Energy', and interestingly, when I woke after having dozed off, it was playing the next track in the library called '7.83 Hz Schuman resonance, activate pineal gland, and 90Hz well-being and balance'. After a short while, and of its own accord, it stopped mid-track and moved on to the next track in the library called 'Healing Harmonics Chakra' by Taos Winds. I thought this was strange, so I looked at when each meditation track had stopped and moved to the next track. The first track had changed after 44 minutes, and the second track had changed after 11 minutes. The meditation tracks were all in sequence in a playlist, so maybe it was caused by a break in relaying the tracks through the internet. I don't know. It's strange as this doesn't usually happen. During the first track, before drifting off to sleep, I felt a vibration in localised spots under my body. I was lying on my back. It seemed to move from place to place. When I woke during the second track, I felt the vibration again. I also felt pressure in my third eye area, which I often feel in that spot. It was a pineal gland activation track, so it's not too surprising to feel my third eye responding. Warick is touching my right cheek now in agreement. It's possible Warick, or other loving spirits, put together a compilation of music and healing energy activities to help me get over this virus infection. Warick just touched my right cheek twice agreeing with me. They are so amazingly clever! I'm so lucky and appreciative to have them in my life.

29 July 2021

Sometimes I wonder with all the Kundalini and other types of spirit activity that went on last year, whether I have actually awakened, but don't know it. I do know for certain I'm more attuned to being 'in the moment' now, particularly when I'm in nature. It's like I notice everything.

Warick was quite active with me last night. When I woke, I felt him touch my right cheek and then started to feel pressure in the forehead where my third eye is. I felt pressure through the bridge of my nose and down into my throat and chest. I also felt a strong pressure pushing up from my cervix and a tingling of energy around my feet. It was like my chakras at the top of my body were pushing down, and my root chakra was pushing up, with energy around my feet and the top of my head. The first time this happened, it was very strong and distinct, and lasted for about ten minutes. As this was occurring, I acknowledged in my mind the different sensations, and tried to stay focused through the third eye as though I was looking at a spot directly in front of me. It was an amazing experience. I couldn't help thinking to myself, *Is this finally it? Am I awakened and using my chakra abilities to be able to tune into Spirit?* Nothing further happened. These sensations did occur again, however—a couple of times but to a lesser degree. The sensations weren't as strong. I get the feeling that Warick is gradually helping me get my chakras connected and working, to enable engagement with the spirit dimension in a more direct and fulfilling way using my upper chakras. He is also still working on the ability to move my facial features. On the night of 27 July, I felt Warick take relatively firm control of my lower jaw while moving it around. He has also opened my mouth before, and made my lips smile, but when this happened it was very slow and gentle. He wasn't rough at all, but it was the firmest I've felt him when taking control. I thought it was great. As you know, I get impatient with how slow this is all going, but I understand it's probably so my body—and conscious mind in particular—become accustomed to all the sensations Warick is causing in a nice, non-threatening way.

Around five thirty this morning, I heard in my left ear a very clear and quite loud tone. It was of medium pitch. I look forward to the day when maybe this turns into a *'Good morning'* instead of a single tone, but I also appreciate and love it the way it is. Just knowing a spirit is dropping in and trying to communicate with me is enough.

Something I forgot to mention—on Monday I was contacted about a job interview I was hoping to get, and yesterday I was contacted about another interview I was also hoping to get. I couldn't help but wonder if this is what the 11:11 signs I've been seeing on the weekend, were all about. I had the first interview yesterday, which I think went pretty well. This was a part-time opportunity. They are only just getting a new consultancy area up and running, so it's more likely to be occasional work, which means I still need a full-time gig. The other interview is my preferred full-time role, which is next week. Fingers crossed I knock their socks off and get the job!

5 August 2021

I find on most days at the moment, at around two in the afternoon, I'm really tired and looking for a sleep. Often, I lie down and do a meditation. I feel a bit flat. It could be the job situation playing on my mind. I'm waiting to hear the outcome of the 'ideal' job I was interviewed for this week. I really hope I get it. I just might also be needing a really good rest and break from work, as I haven't had a proper holiday since before COVID started. Another thing playing on my mind, is I hope that a publisher is going to want to publish these journals. From a personal perspective, this is what matters the most to me at the moment. Ray and I are also wanting to help the family in Indonesia kick off their own tourist driving business in Bali, which will need to wait until I secure my next job.

Last night, I had a really interesting dream where I think Elder visited me. He said that John and I were part of the 'fly away children group'. This is not quite the right wording. He said these children don't focus on what's most important by way of love and other serious matters, but instead want to experience life to the fullest, and chase their desires. I knew what he was saying was important. This was our background in former lives. I suppose to some extent it has been carried into this life. After the dream, I really struggled to remember the exact words he used, which made perfect sense at the time. It disturbed my sleep, saying them over and over in my mind. By the time this morning came around, I remembered the concept he was trying to get across, but not the exact words. Next time this happens, I need to get up and write the words down in the middle of the night. It's the first time Elder has met me in a dream like that and talked with me about me and John.

8 August 2021

I'm conscious that I'm edging closer to the end of this journal. Just like the first one, it's also coinciding with the timing of my birthday. Today I gave the pendulum and free handwriting a go. Warick was happy to use the pendulum and touched my cheek when I asked him to confirm this. The answers didn't involve strong swings of the pendulum, but they were clear. The free handwriting also seemed to happen pretty easily. As I went through this process, I saw shadow shapes move around the notebook as I asked the questions.

Questions to Warick using the pendulum:

- Have I fully awakened already? No
- Is awakening a part of my life contract? Yes
- Am I supposed to use psychic and medium abilities when awakened? Yes
- Is publishing the *AWAKENING* journals a part of my life contract? Yes
- Does Source want the masses to read the *AWAKENING* journals? Yes
- Does Source want humanity to know that their soul continues? Yes
- Is their knowing this a part of humanity's evolution? Yes
- Will there be widespread knowledge of the existence of the soul, which is proven in my lifetime? No
- Is communicating the *AWAKENING* journals, in many different creative ways, a part of my life contract? Yes
  o Written? Yes
  o Art? Yes
  o Music? Yes
  o Audio? Yes

- Will I travel the world talking to people about my experiences with Spirit as recorded in the *AWAKENING* journals? Yes
- Is meeting John a part of my life contract? Yes
- Will John continue to be a part of my awakening journey? Yes
- Will I continue to be a part of John's awakening journey? Yes
- Will I be offered the job I was interviewed for last week? Yes

Free handwriting questions and answers:

- What is your name? Warick
- Why are you here? Love
- What is my life's purpose? Writing
- About what? Spirit
- Am I fully awakened? No
- Will I be? Yes
- When? July 2024
- July 2024? Yes
- Will a publisher want to publish the *AWAKENING* journals? Yes
- What is the name of the publishing company? Lewelyn
- How old are you? 1,003
- 1,003? Yes
- Am I also 1,003? Yes

Continued journal entry

I'm seeing shadow shapes around me now on a daily basis. I often notice them in the bathroom, while watching TV, and when outdoors in nature. I'd say they are with me most of the time, but not always, and I still mostly see the shape with two dots and streaking lines. I also see other shapes, or what's like whisps of smoke, but the two dots and lines form is the most prevalent and is the one that will, at times, come in front of my vision to let me know it's there. I also often experience pressure on one side of my head or the other throughout the day, which is sometimes accompanied by a clear tone of different pitches, which lasts for ten seconds or more. Just about every night, I experience Warick's energy moving about my face and communicating with me through pulse sounds, particularly when I wake early in the morning. On occasion during the night or early morning, he still makes my face smile. Yesterday, while doing a few short third eye awakening meditations, I experienced tingling and a holding sensation around my feet and calves. I also experienced energy move up through my root chakra and through the other chakras to my head. Occasionally, I experience complete peace.

I'm getting more familiar with the sensations associated with my solar plexus, heart and throat chakras. The solar plexus is like a clear surge of energy moving up from just under the base and middle of my rib cage. It moves up through my chest to my throat. It has a particular strength about it, and what I can only describe as intentional drive with a sense of urgency. What I feel from the heart chakra, is a surge of intense emotion. I've written about it before, but I have managed to bring this feeling on myself, when remembering all sorts of lovely experiences with Warick that are very special to me. I don't find doing this easy. More often than not, when I've attempted it, I've found it easier to use my mind to think loving thoughts. The difference when the heart chakra is involved, is that you feel the emotion, rather than just knowing it. With the throat chakra, I often experience what I can only describe as an urge to talk. Like what occurs when you're wanting to break into a conversation. Your voice box and surrounding muscles tense up. Sometimes I get a slight tickle in this area as well. Yesterday, when doing the third eye activation meditation, I also experienced a very distinct energy vibration around the back of my head. It was quite strong. Not a very fast vibration. More of a medium pace that I could also just hear. Collectively, this tells me I'm still progressing. I love that I experience these things in a very real way. It's wonderful! I absolutely love it. I look forward to the continued diverse array of things that Spirit does. It never ceases to amaze me. I'm very grateful for this happening.

9 August 2021

Last night, Warick woke me by vibrating in front of my face. I love it when he does this. It's a very gentle way to wake me up. When I rolled over, the clock said it was 1:11 in the morning. I immediately smiled, thinking Spirit was giving me a message. When I checked in with Warick this morning about the possible significance of seeing 1:11 am, he agreed—via use of the pendulum—that it was a sign that I'm on the right path, and to keep going. I said when I saw 1:11 I thought about the book being published and asked if this helped to manifest it actually happening, to which he agreed. Using the pendulum, Warick also said, 'Yes' to those who interviewed me, wanting to now contact my referees and offering me the job. I hope he's right. This has been playing on my mind, and I should hear something from them today or tomorrow.

I may have mentioned this before, but something I often do when Warick touches my right cheek to let me know he is there, is I use the back of my hand to gently touch my cheek with my fingers in the spot where Warick's energy has just been. I often feel, and can hear, his energy when I do this, particularly when I do it slowly and am expressing a feeling of love for Warick. Just lovely. It confirms in my mind that Warick's energy is in my face. A gesture of endearment between us.

Last night, I experienced the beginnings of energy connections through my chakras and face; however, they didn't progress. I kept drifting off to sleep and was mentally restless. I didn't sleep well. Several times Warick made pulse sounds, one of which sounded like a musical tone, which I've heard before. It sounds like an electric musical tone. At one stage, when I rolled over, I experienced a very clear and quite loud single tone in my left ear. I said, 'Hi. Thanks for trying to communicate.' I also asked Spirit not to give up on me because I can't understand them. I also experienced a pulse of energy move from my third eye down through my throat chakra, my heart chakra, and into my solar plexus area. I found this really interesting. It must be my third eye communicating something to my soul, which supposedly is at the solar plexus chakra. I'd love to know what it meant. I feel like a little kid around grown-ups saying, 'So what does that mean? What's that?' and bombarding them with questions as my mind is curious about things. I pretty much always get ignored. Every now and then, they give me a snippet of information to help me understand in terms that I'm able to grapple with, at my junior stage of Spirit engagement development. Just like a little kid. I find it entertaining just watching what the grownups are doing, even if I don't understand it. It makes me laugh. What a crazy situation this is! One that I wouldn't trade in for the world.

I've just had the most wonderful session with Jane Hall. I decided to see her myself, and to not go ahead with sitting in a circle with Jane, John and Jules because it never seems to be the right time, and because I wanted to close the loop given the session had been paid for as it was part of a program. I can feel a slight pressure in my left ear extending to my voice box now, suggesting Warick or another spirit is with me. I went to the session with Jane today with no expectations. I also put no thought into what might be useful to talk about. Firstly, we chatted about what is happening in the world with the COVID situation. Jane said it will be 2026 before the world, as we knew it in 2019, returns. I suspect she's right. We recapped on where we got up to the last time I saw her. How I've felt anxious about sitting in a circle, not knowing what it's for, and frightened that nothing may happen, which I feel would be letting everyone down. I said how Warick is still with me, and how things have still been happening, including how I've been experiencing things with my chakras. I said how just the other night, I felt a pulse of energy go from my eye chakra, through my throat and heart chakra, to my solar plexus. I said how I've wondered if a message was being sent to my soul from my eye chakra. I also said how I've been wondering if my third eye is open, and I just don't know it. Jane said that, based on the way I was speaking, she definitely thinks my third eye is open. I said I often experience pressure in the third eye area when watching significant news events on TV, or at other random times. I said I've assumed it's Warick dropping in or developing my third eye capability but have also wondered if it's my third eye working or drawing my attention to something. Jane said that when we are first awakening, our senses are highly attuned to all the new stimuli we are experiencing, and that our bond with our guides is very close. We are so used to them helping us to wake up by stimulating the senses, that we tend to think everything we experience is them, and we tend to miss things when it is us at work. We talked about how to use our abilities when we feel pressure in the third eye. Jane used a picture hanging on her wall as a tool to demonstrate and practise with me. It was a painting of what looked to be human tribal figures in different colours dancing in a circle, and a vine of some sort connecting them. There were also what looked to be lotus flowers and leaves on the vine. In the centre, was a blue dove flying with a twig and leaves in its beak. Jane stood in the middle of the room and said, 'You need to set the intent when looking at it, to say if what you see is for someone else or yourself. When I look at it for me, my attention is drawn to a lotus flower, which looks like it has an egg in the middle.' As she was talking, I had already immediately been drawn to the bird in the middle. My logical brain discarded the thought, as it's the middle of the picture where people's eyes generally look to see what is being featured. My mind came back to what Jane was saying. She said, 'You have to put aside your logical thinking mind and instead go with what you feel. It's like unravelling something, where you trust what initially stands out to you, but then keep querying what else you are seeing, feeling, thinking, and picking up through your "clairs". With each thing, keep going, and the next thing will occur to you.' Jane asked me to look at the picture with the intention of it being for Jane. Mentally, I struggled with this, because I had already been focused on the bird, so we went with that. She asked a series of questions, and after each answer she probed for the next thing that I noticed about the bird, and what that meant to me. It went like this:

- What stands out? The bird
- What does it tell you? Free and flying
- What else do you notice? It's blue, which is my favourite colour
- What else? It has a broken wing

How do you relate this to me? Because each time we've met, you've talked about how terribly persecuted you were in past lives. It really bothered me and stuck with me. I want you to be free and to fly. I want to help you. Jane said she still feels persecuted to some degree in this life. Tears were starting to well in my eyes. I said the twig in the bird's beak, and its flight, were a sign that in this lifetime you are starting to mend and are on your way. I then asked Jane directly, 'Do you feel like you are mending and on your way?' To which she responded, 'Yes.'

It was so clear to me I was supposed to tell Jane this. To let her know just how much her past life persecutions, and the damage it had done to her, had upset me. Also, how strongly I felt about wanting to help her. It also proved to me that my third eye is indeed open. I told her how much I appreciated her helping me to realise this, for teaching me how to tune in when I feel pressure in my third eye, to see what I feel and experience with my 'clairs', and to keep probing to unravel all that I should see. While with Jane, I saw shadow shapes around me and felt pressure on and off in my left and right ears. What's important is that I learned to put my logical brain aside and see what I feel.

I told Jane about an interesting experience I had last night while watching one of Joanna Lumley's series about places in the United Kingdom where she took the viewers to a house of significance in a small village. As she walked up to the gate, she gave nothing away as to the owner of the house, or its significance to the village. When I looked at the front gate, the word 'Potter' immediately came to mind. At the time, I wasn't wondering who lived there. Then I thought 'Harry Potter', and immediately discarded the thought, as surely this couldn't be right. Then Joanna said this was the home of 'Beatrix Potter', the famous children's book writer. I couldn't believe it! There was no way I could have known this. Incredible! Literally seconds before she said this, I received the word 'Potter' in my mind. Jane said, this was an example of my claircognizance ability, where words just drop into your mind ahead of finding something out.

I mentioned to Jane how lately I've felt strongly that the *AWAKENING* books should be communicated in a range of creative ways—written, audio, music, and art. I thanked her for referring me to Marie, who is going to sketch my spirit guides. I also told her that lately I've been really curious about native American Indian music. Not modern, but really old native American Indian music. This reminded Jane of a link I sent her to beautiful meditation music, which she said she really likes. This made me think about a wonderful, very old, native American Indian music track that I first came across when exploring their music. It's called 'Heal Your Soul' by Ancestral Way Music. I said to Jane that I'd send her the link. It was later, when I was driving home, that it occurred to me that I'm supposed to send it to her as one way to help her heal. I've been wondering for months about how I could possibly help her. I think this is one way. As we were talking about native American Indian music, Jane got me to look at a picture hanging above my head. It was a picture of an elderly native American Indian man, wearing a full feather head dress, and the colour purple was glowing above him. Jane said his name is White Eagle, and that Marie had sketched him as Jane's spirit guide. Maybe White Eagle had been working with Warick to get me interested in ancestral native American Indian music, to then send Jane this particular 'Heal Your Soul' song to help her heal.

Today was great. I can now see how Jane can help me. Like Jules, someone with whom I can discuss what I'm experiencing, and learn from, so I can use my psychic and medium abilities better as they switch on. As I drove down the road leaving Jane's, I had a strong sensation in my solar plexus. My soul confirming that what I had just learned about my third eye being open is true, and with me, recognising and celebrating the significance of now being consciously aware of it. It was wonderful to have my soul communicate with me in this way. I feel so happy and peaceful. Today is a very special day. When I got home, of course I had to check with Warick using the pendulum, to which he agreed that my third eye is open but that I'm not yet fully awakened.

10 August 2021

Something I must remember that Jane said, is when I feel the pressure in my forehead, I'm already in the zone, or as she and others say, 'in the power', which means I can move straight on to seeing what I can detect with my 'clairs'. If I'm looking at something, I need to focus on what stands out to me and start to unravel the information I'm getting. Something I noticed yesterday, and I've heard other sources say the same thing, is 'Don't try to immediately interpret the information you're getting.' Warick touched my cheek just now in agreement with this. When Jane asked me questions about the picture I was looking at, it wasn't until the fifth question about what I saw, and what it was telling me, that the pieces came together about how I feel about Jane. My sorrow for all the hurt she has endured during past lifetimes—prosecuted in the most horrible ways for her gifts. She said she's been burned alive, had her throat slit, and was treated like a witch. It broke her, and she has carried that fear and hurt into this lifetime. Ever since Jane told me about these things, I've wanted to help her. I feel her pain. Warick is touching my right cheek now in agreement. It is just like I have felt John's sadness, dread and unhappiness. I sent Jane the link to the soul healing native American Indian song yesterday. Early this morning, I asked Warick if she had listened to it yet. I got a very strong sensation from my solar plexus area, which I think was my soul answering, 'Yes'. I hope it helps her.

11 August 2021

I couldn't help but write this one down. Yesterday, while driving along, a number plate on the car in front stood out to me. I think this message would be for anyone, but just in case it becomes significant to me at a later date, I'm recording it. It was 'YOU:11M', and of course I first focused on the number 11, thinking it may be the sign 11, which I keep seeing, but it also says 'YOU' and '11M', which may mean at some stage I may have 11 million dollars. Wouldn't that solve all my problems! I could afford to help the Indonesian family setup their own business in Bali. I could help Jamie and Alaiza get into their first home. We could pay off our mortgages, and I could stop doing project contract work, and instead, spend my time with family and doing what I love—experiencing Spirit, writing these encounters in journals, publishing and communicating them to the world, travelling the world to talk with people about them, and helping scientists in their efforts to prove that intelligent energy exists, and how it interacts with humans. I'm not greedy, nor driven by wealth, but I do know money can make an incredible difference to what you do with your time on Earth.

Last night, I met up with Elder, Warick and Wolf in meditation. I often use the 'Tibetan Healing Sounds' track by Meditation and Relaxation Music channel on *YouTube* when I'm wanting to see them. I've been offered a benefits manager role with one of the big four consultancy companies. They are happy for me to work four days a week, and one of these days from home, which will enable me to balance my time between Canberra and Kianga. I started to feel anxious about accepting the job, after having made such a poor decision in taking up my last role with the little consultancy company. During the meditation, as usual Elder didn't tell me what to do. It's disappointing that the department where I'd been interviewed for my preferred role, didn't get back to me like they said they would at the start of the week. The big four consultancy company is aware of this opportunity, which is a much longer-term role and a senior level leading change. The pressure is on to make a decision on the benefits manager role. Elder said there may be a reason why the benefits manager role has come through first, and the other outcome is delayed. When he said this, I thought it may be a sign that the benefits manager role, although not appearing to be, may in fact be the better role. I had two interviews with the big four consultancy company a day apart, the second including additional people. I connected really well with all of them. I felt relaxed, happy in their company, and could say what I liked with confidence. By comparison, in the interview for the other role, I connected really well with the two senior people; however, the third person on the panel was a middle manager director level. I sensed he was not at ease with the senior people. He didn't get as involved in the conversation. This doesn't bother me as my role in leading change, always involves working with people who are challenging. That said, his role on the project means we would work very closely together. We would also report to the same person (one of the senior people on the panel), which he may not like. I find people in middle management roles can often be a bit competitive and feel a need to control things. This level of management is a well-known source of resistance needing to be addressed in organisational change management. He stammered a bit when asking his question, and his behaviour during the interview suggested he lacks confidence. It's possible that my bubbly and confident demeanour would end up making him feel over shadowed. His involvement and success in a high-profile project would mean a lot to him because he is a permanent, ongoing staff member. Warick is touching my right cheek several times as I'm writing this, suggesting he agrees with me. And again now.

This morning when I woke, I opened my eyes to find myself staring at a pattern of an assortment of types of native flowers on a cushion. The one that stood out to me was the smaller of the two, which were the same type of flower. It was much smaller, almost sickly looking. It was not as nice or as complete in its form, as the rest of the flowers on the pillow. Using the approach Jane taught me, I kept asking myself, *'What do you see? What does it mean to you?'* Overall, I concluded that it's not as good as the other flowers, not as attractive, nor has it got as many stamens. In its mature stage, its purpose is to spread seed. This one has very few seeds on the head of the flower compared with the other of the same type. Despite this, it still had a role to play. I first related it to myself in the jobs I've had in life—not the best, but I've still had a role to play. But maybe the message is about my quandary in deciding about the roles at hand. The benefits manager role is not the best by way of term of the contract and seniority, but maybe it's the right role for me. Warick just touched my right cheek, I think agreeing with me.

Towards the end of the meditation I did last night, Warick took me to a beautiful place, and made love with me on a stone platform on the edge of a cliff next to a thundering waterfall cascading down the rocks. Absolutely beautiful! We have not been there before.

Website: https://www.awakeningforhumanity.com

YouTube: https://www.youtube.com/@awakeningforhumanity
Facebook: https://www.facebook.com/joanne.banyer.2025/
Instagram: https://www.instagram.com/awakeningforhumanity/

www.ingramcontent.com/pod-product-compliance
Lightning Source LLC
Chambersburg PA
CBHW040257170426
43192CB00020B/2833